They Gave Us
Baseball

For Paul:

Merry Christmas

1992

From your brother Jayph.

JOHN M. ROSENBURG

They Gave Us
Baseball

The 12 Extraordinary Men
Who Shaped the Major Leagues

Stackpole Books

Published by
STACKPOLE BOOKS
Cameron and Kelker Streets
P.O. Box 1831
Harrisburg, PA 17105

Printed in the United States of America

10 9 8 7 6 5 4 3 2 1
First Edition

Photos:
Except where noted, all photos were supplied through the courtesy of the National Baseball Library, Cooperstown, N.Y.
   This book contains several rare and interesting photographs (recently un-covered and catalogued by the New York Public Library) that are believed to have been unpublished previously (pages 2, 22, 54, and 57). Credit:
Spalding Collection
Miriam & Ira D. Wallach Division of Art, Prints & Photographs
The New York Public Library
Astor, Lenox and Tilden Foundations

Cover Photos:
Front (clockwise from top left) Judge Kenesaw Mountain Landis, Babe Ruth, Branch Rickey, Harry Wright, Ty Cobb, Jackie Robinson.
Back (clockwise from top left) William Hulbert, John McGraw, Ban Johnson, John Montgomery Ward, Abraham Mills, Albert Spalding.
All courtesy of National Baseball Library, Cooperstown, N.Y.

Cover design by Tracy Patterson.

Library of Congress Cataloging-in-Publication Data

Rosenburg, John M.
      They gave us baseball : the 12 extraordinary men who shaped the major leagues / by John M. Rosenburg.
         p.   cm.
      Includes index.
      ISBN 0-8117-2305-4
      1. Baseball—United States—History. I. Title.
GV863.A1R62 1989
796.357′0973—dc19
                                                                88-30803
                                                                CIP

With deepest affection to
Rosemarie
my lovely, devoted wife
And to my wonderful children and grandchildren

J. M. R.

Contents

Foreword **ix**

Acknowledgments **xi**

Who Gave Us Today's Major Leagues? **xiii**

1 The Trail Blazer 1

2 A Man of Conviction 4

3 A Critical Step 7

4 The Rookie Who Was All Business 9

5 The Bond 12

6 A Critical Handshake 14

7 The Coup d'Etat 17

8 The Reformer 20

9 The Opportunist 23

10 Beer and Whiskey 25

11 Forgotten 28

12 The Fourth Step 30

13 Slavery or Salvation? 33

14 Ignored 36

15 The Adversary 38

16 A Failed Promise 41

17 The Last Straw 44

18 Revolt 46

19 "A War to the Death" 49

20 An Oversight 52

21 The Model 55

22 "As Good as They Come" 58

23 A New Weapon 60

24 Same Horse, Another Race 63

25 Winners All 65

26 David and Goliath 67

27 The Villain and the Hero 71

28 The Gauntlet Is Thrown 73

29 The Saviour 76

30 The Feud 78

31 Recognition Plus 81

32   Little Napoleon 84

33   The Mythmakers 86

34   The Most of Everything 90

35   Shaded 93

36   The Lone Wolf 96

37   The Czar 99

38   Enter the Judge 101

39   The Czar Falls 103

40   A New Hero 106

41   The Great Compromise 109

42   Round One 113

43   One of a Kind 116

44   The Lesson 119

45   Benched 122

46   The Cardinals Arrive 124

47   The Pawns 128

48   A Sad Ending 131

49   The Rebel 135

50   The King 138

51   The Epic Feat 142

52   The Legacy 145

53   Mr. Baseball 148

54   The Ultimate Weapon 151

55   The Color Line 154

56   The Revolution Begins 156

57   Two Cheeks 159

58   The Barrier is Broken 161

59   The Black Knight 164

60   Last of the Pioneers 168

They Gave Us Today's Major Leagues 171

Index 173

About the Author 177

Foreword

WHILE ATTENDANCE at Major League ballparks has gone from roughly 5-million to more than 52-million since the turn of the century and salaries of ballplayers have soared from an average of a few thousand dollars a year to more than $500,000, professional baseball has not always led a happy, vigorous and/or prosperous life.

Several times, in fact, the game appeared to be doomed; rejected by that ultimate arbiter, the baseball fan.

Baseball's periodic and life-threatening difficulties stemmed from a wide variety of causes, including recessions, corruption, faulty rules, greed, player strikes, several devastating internal "wars" and World Wars I and II.

The purpose of this book is to examine baseball's roots to determine who was most responsible for the game's survival and progress and how and why these individuals helped it evolve to its present state.

While thousands have made contributions to baseball over the years (especially those who paid the price of admission to Major and Minor League ballparks), the evidence shows that today's game owes its continued existence primarily to a handful of men; among them players, club owners, managers and officials. And while some may or may not be known to the reader, all but two are enshrined in the National Baseball Hall of Fame in Cooperstown, New York.

The two who are not, should be, as this book will illustrate.

Acknowledgments

F OR MORE THAN 100 YEARS, scores of writers have set down on paper millions upon millions of words to describe the events and personalities that have contributed to the birth, development and growth of baseball

The efforts of these writers can be found in newspapers, books, magazines, letters and an assortment of records, most of which are housed in public libraries.

Without this material to study and draw upon, putting together a book of this type would hardly be possible.

It is with considerable gratitude, then, that we acknowledge the often painstaking and detailed labors of these many authors.

Of all the material read and re-read while preparing the manuscript for this book, we found the following works to be most helpful:

Baseball And The American Dream, by Joseph Durso; *100 Years of Baseball, The American League Story, The National League Story*, all by Lee Allen; *Baseball* by Robert Smith; *The Baseball Story* by Fred Lieb; *Baseball And Mr. Spalding* by Arthur Bartlett; *American Baseball* (Volumes I and II) by David Quentin Voigt; *Baseball America* by Donald Honig; *Sphere And Ash* by Jacob Morse; *The Unforgettable Season* by G. H. Fleming; *Judge Landis and 25 Years Of Baseball* by J. G. Taylor Spink; *Hardball* by Bowie Kuhn; *Ty Cobb* by Charles C. Alexander; *The Glory of Their Times* by Lawrence S. Ritter; *The American Diamond* by Branch Rickey with Robert Riger; *My Life In Baseball: The True Record* by Ty Cobb with Al Stumpf; *The History Of Baseball* by Allison Danzig and Joe Reichler; *Branch Rickey* by Arthur Mann; *My Thirty Years In Baseball* by John McGraw; *The Real McGraw* by Mrs. John McGraw; *America's National Game* by Albert G. Spalding; *Babe* by Robert Creamer; *Baseball* by Harold Seymour; and *A. G. Spalding And the Rise of Baseball* by Peter Levine.

Additional information and background material were drawn from such sources as the Reach, *Spalding* and *Sporting News Baseball Guides, American Heritage Magazine, Sporting Life*, various and numerous newspapers, and the "Spalding Collection" and "Harry Wright Collection," held by the New York Public Library.

Among the individuals most helpful to the author were Patricia Kelly, Tom Heitz and Bill Deane at the National Baseball Hall of Fame and Museum in Cooperstown, New York, and various staff members at the New York, Philadelphia, Paoli and Chester county libraries.

To all of these competent and patient people, go our heartfelt thanks.

J. M. R.

Who Gave Us Today's Major Leagues?

WHATEVER YOUR DEPTH of interest in Major League baseball, have you ever wondered:

- Who established the professional player and team?
- Who established the National League?
- Who established Organized Baseball and the law that governs it?
- Who established the principle of player's rights and the first player's union?
- Who established team defense and team offense?
- Who established the American League?
- Who was the game's greatest player?
- Who established the home run?
- Who established the balance of power among Major League teams?
- Who rid the game of corruption?
- Who broke baseball's "color line"?
- Who forced baseball to expand?
- Who contributed most to baseball?

The 12 men whose careers and achievements are covered in the main text and, for quick reference, are listed on the final page.

1 The Trail Blazer

WILLIAM HENRY WRIGHT, a jeweler by trade, was in his early 20s when he began to look to baseball as a profession.

In 1863, for example, he took up a collection for what was advertised as a "benefit" game. His share of the "benefits" came to $29.65.

Harry Wright, as he was known to family, friends and fans, was born in England on January 10, 1835, the son of a professional cricket player.

The Wrights moved to New York City when he was but 18 months old, his father taking a job as the resident professional of the St. George Cricket Club on Staten Island. By the time he was fully grown, at 5 feet 10 inches tall, Harry had become an excellent cricket player.

By that time, too, Alexander Cartwright, Jr., and his committee of New York Knickerbockers had set down new and different rules for the latest sporting craze in America, "base ball."

Since the practice field for the St. George Club was in Hoboken, New Jersey, near fields used by the Knickerbockers, it was only natural for Harry Wright and his two younger brothers, George and Sam, to become interested in the game. Before long, all three were playing baseball as well as cricket. Harry, in fact, began playing for the Knickerbockers in 1858. Later, he and his brothers played for several other teams.

During this period, some 60 clubs were members of the National Association Of Baseball Players, an organization founded to regulate the game on a uniform basis.

Among the Association's rules was one that proclaimed that all players must be amateurs.

It was as a cricket professional in the late 1860s, however, that Harry was introduced to sports-minded Cincinnati, the self-styled "hog-butchering capital of the world." At $1,200 a year, Harry became the coach of the Union Cricket Club. But cricket was not as popular as baseball in Cincinnati. This was underlined by the fact that the Buckeyes, a local baseball team, outdrew the cricket team by a wide margin.

The success of the Buckeyes prompted a Cincinnati group to field a baseball team in 1867, with Harry Wright as player-manager at the same salary. This, Wright's first diamond squad, was made up of local amateurs. The team did fairly well, but lost to the Buckeyes and the touring Washington Nationals, a team of Government "workers" led by one of the most sensational players of the day, Harry Wright's younger brother, George.

After the season, Harry made it clear to his employers that if they hoped to at least beat and outdraw the Buckeyes, they had better sign a

1

This rare photo of Sam Wright (left) and his son Harry was taken while both were employed as resident "pros" at the St. George Cricket Club on Staten Island, New York, sometime in the 1850s. New York Public Library, Spalding Collection.

few professionals. After all, he pointed out, some of the Buckeye players, like those of the Washington Nationals and other teams, were getting salaries for phantom jobs.

The new president of the club—a Cincinnati lawyer and local merchant named Aaron B. Champion—and the board of directors were quick to agree. As a result, the team that began the 1868 season had six professionals (all disguised in one way or another) in the lineup.

It also enjoyed the use of refurbished grounds, thanks to Champion's energetic fund-raising activities.

And to add to the bewhiskered club's dash and allure, the shrewd Wright had flashy new uniforms made by a person later identified as a "female tailor."

To the astonishment and delight of all, the uniforms featured knickers instead of long pants. And with what proved to be a classic and historic touch, Wright added a pair of bright-red woolen stockings. (The spectacular uniforms were designed and made by a local woman named Margaret Truman whose sister, Mary, married the Red Stockings pitcher, Asa Brainard.)

The uniforms and improved play of the Red Stockings paid off. Not only did the Red Stockings outdraw the Buckeyes at the gate, they whipped them on the diamond. The Buckeyes then reverted to a strictly amateur team, with the result that the Red Stockings soon became the toast of the town.

Harry Wright had made his point.

If the Cincinnati baseball club wanted a winning ball team, it had no choice but to search out the best talent it could find. And the way to get that talent in uniform, he made clear, was to offer a contract that promised cold cash.

In 1868, however, this was heresy. Turning publicly professional, most argued, would never be accepted by the community. Furthermore, it was a serious violation of the National Association rules to pay anyone—directly or indirectly—to play baseball.

Still, Wright insisted, the rules were rarely enforced because the Association was too weak to enforce them. And, he said, for the Association to pose as an "amateur" organization year after year amounted to hypocrisy!

Finally, during the winter of 1868–69, an enthusiastic Aaron Champion and his directors agreed with Wright and decided to go all out for a winning team. Two major steps were taken:

- Champion raised funds by selling $15,000 worth of stock in the club.
- Wright was authorized to hire the most skillful players he could locate.
- By the spring of 1869, Wright had nine of the best under contract.

With that bold, defiant, unheard-of-move, Harry Wright had begun to blaze the trail that led to the stormy development of today's Major Leagues.

Harry Wright, the man who started it all—including the knee pants and long stockings.

2 A Man of Conviction

HARRY WRIGHT'S SIGNING of the first all-professional team stirred up a beehive of discussion in baseball-minded America.

There were those who applauded the move and those who shook their heads in sorrow. And there were those who insisted that gate receipts alone could never support a baseball team.

By 1869, however, the muscular, 34-year-old Wright had been in baseball for more than 10 years. A veteran of the diamond, he knew how to play; he knew how to manage; he knew how to promote the game and he knew how to teach.

Above all, Harry Wright was guided by two convictions: (1) Americans would grow to like baseball more than any other sports activity then in existence, and; (2) Fans would gladly pay a reasonable price to see a well-trained team and an honest, clean exhibition of the game.

Holding fast to those beliefs, Wright vigorously went about preparing for what would be a critical turning point in baseball's evolution. He began by signing his brother, George, to a contract. This was a major coup, for George—a seasoned player 12 years younger than Harry—was the best fielding shortstop in the game and certainly one of the best hitters.

By the opening of the 1869 season, the Red Stockings' lineup looked like this:

> George Wright, shortstop
> Harry Wright, captain,
>   center fielder and relief
>   pitcher
> Asa Brainard, pitcher
> Fred Waterman, third base
> Charles Sweasy, second base
> Charles Gould, first base
> Douglas Allison, catcher
> Andrew Leonard, left field
> Cal McVey, right field
> Richard Hurley, substitute

It was a young team, these Red Stockings of 1869. Next to Harry Wright, Brainard was the oldest at 25. The rest ranged in age from 20 to 23.

And by the standards of the day, they were well paid for their services during the March to November season. George Wright, for example, received $1,400; Harry $1,200; Brainard $1,100, and Sweasy $1,000. The rest each received $800, bringing the total payroll to $9,500.

When all his players were signed, Harry Wright spread the word that the Cincinnati Red Stockings were willing to take on any team in the

The Cincinnati Red Stockings of 1869, the first all-professional team. Seated (left to right) are Andy Leonard, Richard Allison, Asa Brainard, Charles Sweasy; standing are Cal McVey, Charles Gould, Harry Wright, George Wright, Fred Waterman.

nation. All he asked was one-third of the gate receipts when on the road. (At home, arrangements with visiting teams varied.)

While waiting for teams to accept his challenge, Wright, a strong believer in physical fitness, launched a vigorous training program for his players. He also concentrated on strategy and defensive and offensive skills.

Even as a pitcher, Wright was innovative. He was believed to be the first to introduce the "change-up." A tantalizing, slow pitch, the change-up was delivered after a fast one; the purpose being to upset a hitter's timing.

On their first swing east, the club encountered the toughest teams on their schedule and beat them all by substantial margins. They whipped the Brooklyn Atlantics 30 to 11, for example; the Brooklyn Eckfords 24 to 5; the Philadelphia Athletics 27 to 18, and the Washington Nationals 47 to 7. The closest game was a 4 to 2 victory over the Brooklyn Mutuals.

Returning to Cincinnati, the Red Stockings continued to win, beating visitors from all over the West and Midwest.

Looking for new worlds to conquer, Cincinnati went to the West Coast. En route, they beat teams in St. Louis; and when they arrived in San Francisco, they rolled over the three best teams that city had to offer, scoring more than 50 runs in each game and holding their opponents to fewer than 10.

By the time the season was over, the Red Stockings had traveled almost 12,000 miles and played before approximately 200,000 "cranks," or fans. Of the 57 games played, Wright's team won 56 and tied one. During this remarkable winning streak, the team scored 2,395 runs to their opponents' 574.

As expected, George Wright was the team's leading hitter, with a batting average of just over .500 and an astonishing 59 of the team's 169 homers.

The only blemish on Cincinnati's 58-game schedule was the 17–17 tie with the Troy Haymakers. Played in Cincinnati, the game was called off in the fifth inning when the Troy captain argued with the umpire with such vehemence the crowd appeared ready to riot.

Later, it was reported that gamblers had provoked the incident so they wouldn't have to pay off some $17,000 bet on Troy to win. (Although the umpire had forfeited the game to Cincinnati, he was overruled by the Players Association and the game reverted to a tie in the recordbooks.)

The unprecedented victory march of the Red Stockings in 1869 brought Wright and his team not only glory but an avalanche of publicity by a new breed of reporter, the sportswriter.

The team's fame was such that it was greeted by President Grant before defeating the Washington Nationals. And when it arrived home before the trip west, it seemed as if all of Cincinnati turned out to welcome the team.

At a dinner in the Red Stockings' honor, a local lumber mill presented Wright with a remarkable trophy—a baseball bat that was 27 feet long and 18 inches thick. Appropriately, the name of each player was carved into the bat.

And during a toast to the team, Champion touched off a roar of approval when he vowed that "I would rather be President of the Red Stockings than President of the United States!"

Without doubt, the season was a smashing success for Cincinnati's powerful Cinderella team.

Most notable of all, however, was the fact that Harry Wright, a man of convictions, had proved, for the first time, that professional baseball, with its promise of excitement and drama, was a viable enterprise.

3 A Critical Step

T HE EXTRAORDINARY POWER and finesse of the 1869 Cincinnati Red Stockings established clearly that amateurs could not compete on equal terms with an all-professional team.

As a result, several clubs quietly began to copy Harry Wright's formula for success. Despite this, the Red Stockings were able to roll up 27 victories during another eastern tour in 1870 before coming face-to-face with a tough imitator, the Brooklyn Atlantics.

With a crowd of some 9,000 on hand, Wright's team got off to a fast start, scoring three runs in the top of the first inning and another in the third.

It was a typical beginning for the Red Stockings, and thousands in the ballpark were convinced the awesome Cincinnati machine was on its way to racking up its 84th win in 85 games.

To the roaring delight of the Brooklynites, however, the Atlantics rallied, scoring two runs in the fourth inning and two in the sixth to take a 4 to 3 lead.

But, the battle was far from over.

Cincinnati came back with a pair of runs in the seventh, while the Atlantics scored again in the eighth to create a 5–5 tie.

In the bottom of the ninth, the Atlantic put runners on first and second with one out as the Brooklyn fans screamed and begged for the hit that would end the Red Stockings' long string of victories.

Despite a mighty swing of the bat, however, the best the next Brooklyn hitter could do was raise a weak pop fly to George Wright at short.

Wright got under the ball and set himself for the catch as the runners held tight to their respective bases.

At the last second, however, George deliberately dropped the ball, scooped it up and threw to Fred Waterman for a force-out at third base.

Waterman promptly fired to second baseman Charlie Sweasy for another force to complete the first doubleplay of its kind; a play that eventually led to today's infield fly rule.

With the inning ended, the Atlantics' captain, Bob Ferguson, though disappointed, indicated he was satisfied to settle for a tie.

The crowd promptly poured onto the field.

But Harry Wright, with Aaron Champion at his side, protested vigorously to both the umpire and Ferguson.

"The game is not over!" Wright yelled repeatedly above the din of the joyous Brooklyn fans. "The rules say that as long as there's daylight, we've got to play extra innings until the tie is broken!"

Finally, after a long and heated discussion, it was agreed that the game should go on. With some difficulty the crowd was shooed off the field and the umpire signaled "Play Ball!"

The tenth inning was scoreless. In the eleventh, with daylight fading rapidly, the Red Stockings came to bat and scored two runs.

Again, the Atlantics refused to quit.

In the bottom of the 11th, they scored three runs on a single, a wild pitch and an error to bring an abrupt and dramatic end to the game and the Red Stockings' winning streak.

Back at his hotel, Champion sent a telegram to club members in Cincinnati. It read:

"Atlantics eight. Cincinnati seven. The finest game ever played. Our boys did nobly but fortune was against them. Eleven innings. Though beaten not disgraced."

During the rest of that season, the Red Stockings lost five more games as attendance dropped off sharply. Clearly, their fickle followers no longer regarded Wright's team as "number one."

When the club's board of directors met late in the fall, a crestfallen Aaron Champion was ousted as President. The reason: The Red Stockings had failed to show a profit after two seasons of play.

Since the directors then let it be known there would be no pay increases for the players in 1871, other clubs quickly bid for their services. Soon, they were gone.

The dissolution of the Cincinnati club, however, failed to shake Wright's faith in the notion that professional baseball had a bright and prosperous future.

He made that quite clear by quickly accepting an offer to put together another all-pro team in a city that called itself the "hub of the universe" — Boston.

In moving from Cincinnati to Boston, Wright took with him first baseman Charlie Gould, right fielder Cal McVey and his sensational shortstop, brother George.

He also took something else to Boston: the red stockings.

Thus, by donning the indelible part of the Cincinnati uniform that brought such pointed glory to the cause of the professional player, the Boston squad became known as the "Boston Red Stockings."

During the winter of 1870-71, the breach between the professionals and amateurs widened rapidly. By the following spring, in fact, Harry Wright and his fellow "pros" had ended their relationship with the National Association.

Overnight — on March 17, 1871 — Wright and his friends established another organization with an unmistakable name:

"The National Association of PROFESSIONAL Base Ball Players."

With J.W. Kerns in the chair as its first President, the new Association voted into membership the following clubs:

> Boston, Red Stockings
> Chicago, White Stockings
> New York, Mutuals
> Washington, Olympics
> Cleveland, Forest City
> Troy (N.Y.), Haymakers
> Fort Wayne (Ind.), Kekiongas
> Rockford (Ill.), Forest City

Since the managers and directors of each of these teams vowed to fill their rosters with professionals, the amateurs were abruptly shunted aside. And the national organization they held together for 12 years soon faded out of existence.

For Harry Wright, baseball's first professional manager of an all-professional team, it was a second and important step in what would prove to be a long and illustrious career.

For baseball, it was also a second step; a critical step, in fact, that would nudge the game closer to development of the Major Leagues.

4 The Rookie Who Was All Business

H ARRY WRIGHT KNEW precisely where to go to try and sign the one man he needed most to make the Boston Red Stockings a winner. After all, he and brother, George, had come in contact with scores of ballplayers as they toured the country with both the Cincinnati club of 1869 and other teams. And they knew then—just as managers know today—that a baseball team cannot hope to be successful without good pitching.

Since each team carried only one full-time pitcher, they could hardly forget Rockford, home of the Forest City club. For it was the Rockford hurler who handed the touring Washington Nationals their only defeat in 1867 with George Wright in the lineup.

And it was the same pitcher who beat the Cincinnati Red Stockings in 1870, with both Wrights in the lineup.

His name was Albert Goodwill Spalding.

Spalding was born on September 2, 1850, in Byron, Illinois. He was the son of prosperous farmers, but his father died when he was nine years old, leaving his mother, Harriet Spalding, to rear the family.

Spalding got involved in baseball while boarding with a relative in Rockford, Illinois, and working as a grocery clerk for $3 a week. Away from home for the first time, the 13-year-old Spalding was lonely and homesick.

"The only solace I had," he recalled years later, "the only bright skies for me in those dark days of utter loneliness were when I could go out to the commons to watch the other fellows play baseball."

His vantage point, he said, was deepest center field. One day, a player hit the ball solidly and drove it over the center fielder's head.

Instinctively, Spalding jumped to his feet, made a short run and caught the ball. It must have been an impressive catch, for he joined the team the next day.

Spalding first attracted attention as a player when he pitched for the Rockford Pioneers. At the time, he was a gangly 15-year-old schoolboy. Handsome and solidly built at 6 foot, 1 inch, the right-hander was easily the star of his all-schoolboy team.

The scrappy and talented Pioneers challenged two other teams in Rockford—the Forest Citys and the Mercantiles. Both boosted lineups of adults. And both tried to ignore the Pioneers, feeling it was beneath them to step on the same diamond with teenagers.

The Mercantiles, the weaker of the two teams, finally gave in to the taunts and badgering of local fans and agreed to take on the Pioneers.

It was a mistake.

With Spalding doing the hurling, the Pioneers humiliated the condescending Mercantiles 26 to 20. As a result, Spalding and an infielder named Ross Barnes accepted invitations to join the Forest Citys.

With Spalding doing most of the pitching, the Forest City club went on to whip virtually every rival in their area of Illinois except one—the Excelsiors of nearby Chicago.

When Spalding was 17, the Excelsiors staged a baseball tournament at Dexter Park, a Chicago racetrack. Rockford was one of the teams invited to participate.

The big attraction was to be the final game of the tournament between the supposedly superior Excelsiors and the Washington Nationals.

That game would also mark the end of the Nationals' victorious 2,400-mile tour—a tour during which the Nationals went undefeated and humbled teams in Columbus, Cincinnati and St. Louis by such scores as 90 to 10, 88 to 12, 113 to 26 and 53 to 26.

To warm up for the anticipated climax with the Excelsiors, the Nationals agreed to play the Forest Citys, even though the two school-boys, Spalding and Barnes, were to be in the lineup.

To the amazement of the large crowd that had paid a 25¢ admission to see the game, Rockford won 29 to 23.

The following day, to make the Rockford victory over the Nationals even sweeter, the Nationals trimmed the Excelsiors 49 to 4 in the "feature" game of the tournament. This touched off a week-long celebration in Rockford for the town's new national "Champions" and "the best pitcher in the world."

Four years later, Harry Wright journeyed from Boston to Rockford and signed Spalding, second baseman Ross Barnes and outfielder Fred Cone to Red Stockings contracts. In doing so, however, Wright cautioned that fans in the east had not yet fully accepted professionalism and he preferred that the players not discuss their contracts with anyone.

Spalding, according to his memoirs, objected. The Chicago White Stockings, he pointed out, had advertised for "skilled" ballplayers with a flat offer of $1,200 a year. To pretend that the great Wright brothers, Cal McVey and other famous players would represent the Red Stockings as

Albert Goodwill Spalding, professional baseball's first major pitching star and Harry Wright's most important disciple.

amateurs and play ball for "healthful and philanthropic reasons" wouldn't fool anyone, he argued.

Spalding said he intended to make a career of baseball. He added that baseball was a business and the sooner it was recognized as such the better for all concerned.

Since Wright had long ago come to this same conclusion, he agreed.

And when the 1871 season opened, Harry Wright knew that in Al Spalding he had a promising rookie on the roster who was all business and a man after his own heart.

5 The Bond

AL SPALDING'S ARRIVAL in Boston in 1871 as a bona fide professional player in baseball's first bona fide professional league could not have been more auspicious.

He began by going undefeated in 21 games — 20 victories and one tie. As a team, the Red Stockings won 22, tied one and lost 10 during the Association's shortened embryo season.

Each year thereafter, Spalding's pitching record got better. In 1872, for example, Spalding won 36; in 1873, 41; in 1874, 52; and in 1875, 56. Overall, in that five-year span, his record was 205–55 and included one tie.

When he wasn't pitching, Spalding played the outfield. In fact, the records show that Spalding was in the lineup during virtually every one of the 288 games the Red Stockings played from 1871 through 1875.

Without a doubt, Spalding was the greatest star of this period.

In reviewing the Red Stocking's lineup before the start of one season, a newspaper noted that "as a pitcher, Spalding has no superior, being very fast as well as very cunning. He is the tallest man in the nine and a powerful batsman. Spalding has an honorable record as a ball tosser, and he and McVey as pitcher and catcher can work together better than any two men in the country. . . ."

But it was more than Spalding's skill as a player that made him a celebrity. He was not only tall and good looking, he was intelligent, articulate and polite. He was also patient with the groups of small boys who followed him around the streets of Boston and elsewhere.

Furthermore, he shunned gamblers, stayed out of saloons and trained hard; attributes that were admired by many.

Henry Chadwick, the first and foremost baseball writer of the day, made the point, in fact, that "the intelligent and gentlemanly" Spalding was a credit to the game.

"Both on and off the baseball field, he conducts himself in a manner well calculated to remove the public's bad impression as to professional ball tossers, created by swearing, gambling specimens who form the black sheep of the flock," Chadwick wrote. "In fact, he has sense enough to know that fair and manly play, and honorable and faithful service are at least as much the essential of a professional ballplayer as is skill in the field and at bat."

Young Spalding, of course, had the good fortune to enter the world of professional baseball as a disciple of Harry Wright.

Still young and vigorous at 37 when Spalding played for him, Wright was a hard-working, diligent and innovative manager.

He was undoubtedly the first to instill in his players an attitude of "professionalism." He insisted, for example, that the Red Stockings be on time for all practice sessions and games. He also demanded that they be in top physical condition and urged them not to drink or smoke.

And while he constantly sought new ways to beat his opponents, Harry Wright stuck by his creed: Give the customers a well-played game with an all-out effort to win.

Wright, more than any other manager in baseball, espoused the doctrine of clean baseball and harped constantly on the need to "elevate" the game. Early in 1872, for instance, he chastised the manager of the Philadelphia Athletics for hanging the Association's first championship banner in a saloon.

In the same vein, Wright abhorred gamblers and drunks and dishonesty in any form. (On religious grounds, he also was opposed to playing baseball on Sunday, a position that brought him into serious conflict with others.)

But Harry Wright was more than a manager on the field. He did all of the front office work. He scheduled games, arranged for transportation, directed the grounds crew, kept the books and handled the advertising, payroll and club expenses.

In all of this, he was observed and assisted by eager, interested and ambitious Al Spalding, his junior by 15 years.

After a brief and successful tour of Canada in 1872, Spalding and Wright began to hint to newsmen and others that they might take baseball to England.

Naturally, such a possibility generated a lot of publicity, most of it favorable.

Finally, it was decided: Even though Spalding, then only 24, had never been out of the country, he was to travel to England and explore the possibility of staging exhibition games at cricket clubs between the Red Stockings and Philadelphia Athletics.

Spalding, who left in January 1874, went well beyond his assigned mission. Without Wright's knowledge or approval, he boldly booked a series of exhibition games and cricket matches in various parts of England. (He also went to France to attempt the same thing but there was no interest.)

Delighted by Spalding's daring promotional coup, Wright quickly made all the arrangements. And in July, a party of 38 left Philadelphia for England, where the A's and the Red Stockings played 14 games, Boston winning eight of them.

The baseball players also took on several cricket teams, beating them all at their own game.

While Wright and Spalding failed to convince the British that baseball could or would replace cricket, the tour was a critical, if not a great financial success.

More important, it helped establish a stong and lasting bond between professional baseball's two earliest and most important pioneers — Harry Wright and Al Spalding.

6 A Critical Handshake

T HE LEAGUE THAT America's professional ballplayers operated for the first time in 1871 began to run into serious problems almost immediately.

One problem stemmed from the decision that the Philadelphia Athletics had the right to fly the "championship streamer" since the team had won 22 games and lost but 7.

Harry Wright's Red Stockings, on the other hand, had won 22 and lost 10.

Wright insisted that since Philadelphia had not completed its schedule and, as a result, played fewer games, the flag belonged in Boston.

Although he lost his protest, Wright got his revenge the following year when the Red Stockings whipped the As 13 to 4 and, according to the newspapers of the day, prompted "half the city" of Boston to take a holiday.

From that point on, Wright's Red Stockings won four pennants in a row with the following seasonal results.

Year	Won	Lost
1872	39	8
1873	43	16
1874	52	18
1875	71	8

Unfortunately, Boston was virtually the only club that could lay claim to any sort of success during this period, and League fortunes went rapidly downhill. The primary problem was that nothing had really changed when the professionals kicked the amateurs out of the national organization.

The poisonous effect of gambling, in fact, seemed to reach new heights as poorly paid, unscrupulous, hard-drinking players often succumbed to the lure of easy money to fix or throw games.

Then, too, the lack of firm schedules and the instability of Association clubs undermined public confidence and ruined chances to build a following.

In one season, to be specific, almost half of the 232-game schedule was canceled as teams either quit or refused to travel for lack of funds.

The playing rules were also far from satisfactory and led to almost endless tinkering. During 1874, the rules committee went so far as to add a tenth man to each team—a move that was dropped quickly.

Ironically, Boston's success created another major problem for the League. While the Red Stockings drew well in Boston and Philadelphia, they failed to do so in other towns because those who rooted for their local heroes grew tired of watching them always lose by lopsided scores. In 1875, Boston's best year, six of the 13 teams on the circuit dropped out.

Unfortunately, no one seemed to be able to do anything to correct matters. No one, that is, until a man named William Hulbert came along.

Although born October 23, 1832, in Berlington Flats in Otsego County, New York, which is not far from Cooperstown, where the National Baseball Hall of Fame and Museum is located, Hulbert spent most of his life in Chicago, a circumstance that once prompted him to say, "I'd rather be a lamp post in Chicago than a millionaire anywhere else."

Not long after graduating from Beloit College, Hulbert went into the coal business and subsequently became a member of the Chicago Board of Trade. He also became an avid baseball fan and accepted an invitation to join the Board of Directors of the Chicago White Stockings.

As a club Director, Hulbert quickly became intimately acquainted with the difficulties confronting the White Stockings and baseball in general.

A colleague once described Hulbert as a man with a "magnificent physique, commanding presence, strong personality and endowed with a powerful intellect, keen logic, and impressive directness of speech. . . essentially a leader among men. . . ."

While he may or may not have been all of these things, the White Stockings' hierachy was impressed enough with Hulbert to offer him the presidency after the club had finished seventh in 1874.

Before he accepted, Hulbert contacted Al Spalding. He told Spalding of the offer and said he was hesitant about taking the post because of all the difficulties confronting baseball.

He then made a bold suggestion. If Spalding would agree to join the White Stockings the following year, he would accept the presidency.

By pitching for Chicago, Hulbert pointed out, Spalding could help correct the game's biggest problem: the imbalance of power within the League.

"You're a Western man, Al," he said. "You belong in Chicago."

When Spalding said he was interested, Hulbert agreed to become President of the Chicago club.

Later, in June, Hulbert traveled to Boston and offered Spalding $2,000 a year and 25 percent of the gate to hurl for the White Stockings in 1876. He also asked Spalding to take on the responsibility of captain and manager of the team.

Since this would amount to more than twice the salary Spalding earned at Boston and represented a great career opportunity, Spalding eagerly accepted.

Then Hulbert made another proposal. Why not sign McVey, Barnes and White, the balance of Boston's "Big Four"?

As it would be in his best interest to build a powerful White Stockings team, Spalding added another name—Adrian Anson, star of the Philadelphia Athletics—and said he would try to sign all four.

The two shook hands.

While it may seem contradictory, that critical handshake launched the first major move to reform and save baseball.

7 The Coup d'Etat

AL SPALDING, utilizing the simple expedient of offering Barnes, McVey, White and Anson healthy increases in pay, had little difficulty persuading the four to sign with Chicago.

Under the rules of the Association, however, players contracted to one team could be expelled for signing a contract with another.

As a result, Hulbert asked the newly acquired White Stockings not to mention the switch to Chicago until after their 1875 contracts expired in October.

Somehow, however, word of the sensational deal reached the ears of Chicago sportswriters and the story soon exploded in print. When approached by Boston reporters, McVey, White and Barnes denied the story. Reached at a later date, Spalding admitted that the Big Four and Anson had agreed to play for Chicago in 1876.

Spalding insisted, however, that he and his teammates would continue to be loyal to Boston for the balance of the year.

Even though the Red Stockings won every home game, most Boston fans could not forgive the "seceders." They booed, hissed and hurled epithets at the Big Four at every opportunity, whether on the diamond or in the streets.

Confronted with the very real possibility that his five new players would be expelled from the Association, Hulbert came up with a startling idea: Why not form a new organization to replace the tottering Association and eliminate the threat of expulsion? Such a move would also offer an opportunity to eradicate the evils that so clearly threatened the life of baseball.

With Spalding's encouragement and help, Hulbert began working on his novel plan in the fall of 1875, racing to have everything in place before the start of the following season. Hulbert's basic concept—revolutionary at the time—boiled down to this: Baseball should be structured as a business and operated by businessmen, not players.

In confidence, Hulbert contacted Harry Wright, the most knowledgeable man in the game, told Wright of his plans, and asked for his ideas and advice.

Wright, by now totally disillusioned with the Association, responded promptly and laid out many of his views. In one letter, for example, Wright said that if baseball clubs were to survive they "must have gate money, to receive gate money they must play games, and to enable them to play games, their opponents must have faith that such games will prove remunerative. . . ."

With Wright's support, Hulbert and Spalding drafted a constitution, then called the backers of the St. Louis, Cincinnati and Louisville clubs to Louisville for a secret meeting that took the better part of a week.

Hulbert pointed out to the Westerners that the only way to rid themselves of Eastern domination, clean up baseball and make the game profitable was to start afresh with a new organization.

His listeners agreed.

A few days later, Hulbert invited backers of four Eastern clubs to a meeting in New York on February 2 at the Grand Central Hotel.

Prior to the general meeting, Hulbert cleverly scheduled one-on-one sessions with representatives of Boston, Philadelphia, Hartford and New York at half-hour intervals. This enabled him to pre-sell his case.

At the main meeting, after asking Morgan Bulkeley of Hartford to act as chairman and Harry Wright as secretary, Hulbert offered a resolution to the assembled group that said in part, "We, the undersigned, lamenting the abuses which have insidiously crept into the exposition of our National Game . . . hereby pledge each other that we will withdraw from the National Association of Professional Baseball Players and we hereby announce that we have this day organized ourselves into a National League of Professional Baseball Clubs."

The resolution was adopted unanimously.

Hulbert's constitution was then introduced. From the clubowners' point of view it was a beautiful piece of legislation, since it seemed to have the potential of solving virtually every problem confronting Major League baseball and the men who would run it.

Hulbert's edict set club entry fees, annual dues and a 50¢ admission charge; gave umpires the authority to throw rowdy players and fans out

William Hulbert brought a revolutionary concept to baseball.

Henry Chadwick, baseball's first full-time reporter, was startled by what happened during the winter of 1875–76.

of the ballpark; called for police protection; prohibited Sunday games; and barred gambling within the confines of the ballyard.

In addition, these key stipulations were built into Hulbert's overall program:

- Each club must be in a city with a minimum population of 75,000 and situated at least five miles from any other League Club.
- A written contract would bind players to a club and the League rules.
- Players expelled by one club would be barred by all.
- Any player found guilty of dishonest play would be thrown out of baseball for life.
- Clubs failing to complete all scheduled games would be expelled.
- The President of the League would chair a five-man Board of Directors, with each Director being a President of a member club.
- A Secretary-Treasurer was to be hired to take charge of all book-keeping and clerical duties.

With minor adjustments, the eight club representatives endorsed all of these rules. Thus, in less than four months, Hulbert, Spalding, Wright and their fellow conspirators had accomplished the following:

- Killed baseball's first Major League.
- Rendered moot the question of whether Anson and the Boston Big Four could be barred from baseball for jumping to Chicago.
- Given birth to the National League.

Sportswriter Henry Chadwick wrote an apt characterization of this development when he heard about it. ". . . a startling coup d'état," he said. But baseball's troubles were far from over.

8 The Reformer

S INCE THE NATIONAL LEAGUE was virtually the sole creation of Will Hulbert, he undoubtedly could have been its first President.

But Hulbert, ever the politician, suggested Morgan Bulkeley, owner of the Hartford club, in an effort to smooth relations with the stronger clubs in the East. The owners, going along with Hulbert, elected Bulkeley President and Nicholas Young as Secretary-Treasurer.

Nine months later, Bulkeley resigned to concentrate on politics and Hulbert became the League's second President.

Among other things, the constitution fashioned by Hulbert gave club owners complete control of the players who once ruled the game. At the same time, it established baseball as a monopoly.

To the delighted owners, this translated into a word they all understood and welcomed: P-R-O-F-I-T!

But the seemingly gold-plated package the New York conferees adopted that February day and evening in 1876 was, after all, nothing more than a few hundred words on paper.

To make the carefully honed body of rules and regulations work, they would have to be enforced, a fact recognized by Hulbert above all others.

The National League's first season got off to a fine start in Philadelphia on Saturday, April 22. Some 3,000 fans turned out to see the Boston Red Stockings nip the A's 6 to 5.

The remaining clubs swung into action the following week, getting the 70-game pennant race fully underway.

As might be expected, the Chicago White Stockings easily won the first National League Championship with a record of 56 wins and 14 losses.

Spalding, who did almost all of the pitching, won 46 of the games for the club he now managed.

During the course of the season, however, the New York Mutuals and the Philadelphia Athletics failed to play all of their scheduled contests. Thus, the power structure of the new League faced its first major crisis.

It didn't last long. Hulbert booted New York and Philadelphia out of the League, a sorry ending to an otherwise fairly successful season.

The following year (1877), Hulbert had another problem on his hands involving last-place Cincinnati.

Si Keck, the Cincinnati owner, claimed he was losing money and failed to pay his League dues. Not only that, he refused to cover his team's expenses for the first trip East. In June, Keck disbanded the club and released the players.

When word of this reached Hulbert, he sent a secret emissary to Cincinnati to sign two of Keck's former players for the Chicago White Stockings; second baseman Joe Hallinan and a slugging left fielder, Charlie Jones, Cincinnati's most popular player.

A month later, a group of Cincinnatians bought out Keck and took over all his obligations so the team could finish its schedule.

Naturally, the new owners wanted their players back. When Hulbert refused, taking the stand that the players had been released, the Cincinnati fans and newspapers set up a howl.

Hulbert was seen as a "vulture" and accused of using his position as President of the League to help the White Stockings win another championship.

Finally, a compromise was struck: Hulbert would keep Hallinan and return Jones.

But the Cincinnati problem was minor compared to the one that cropped up later in the season involving the first-place Louisville Grays.

While the Grays were a dark horse in the spring, pitcher Jim Devlin almost single-handedly carried them to the front with a tremendous performance. Ranked only slightly behind Al Spalding in pitching prowess, Devlin appeared in almost every game and was a consistent winner until the final weeks of the season.

But the Grays and other players were an unhappy lot that summer. League rules allowed clubs to charge them $30 for uniforms and also 50¢ a day for every day they were on the road, rain or shine.

Consequently, the players were prime targets for an approach by various members of the gambling fraternity.

Suspicions were aroused when the Grays, leading Harry Wright's Boston team by a supposedly safe margin, suddenly began to drop games.

Among those who sensed something amiss was the Louisville Vice President, Charles Chase. Chase also noticed an odd thing: Some of his players were receiving an unusual number of telegrams while on the road.

One of these telegrams was intercepted. While partly in code, the message was clear: Games were being lost deliberately on instructions from gamblers.

James Devlin, star pitcher of the Louisville Grays, was one of four players involved in baseball's first major scandal. New York Public Library, Spalding Collection.

Chase called the players into his office and demanded the right to ask Western Union for copies of all telegrams the players had sent and received.

This ploy brought one confession, then another. Soon, Chase had enough evidence to prove the four had conspired with gamblers to throw several games.

He suspended Devlin; the team Captain and shortstop, Bill Craver; left fielder George Hall, and utility infielder Al Nichols.

Boston, with pitcher Tommy Bond winning 40 of the Red Stockings' 42 games, captured the pennant by a comfortable margin. And while this was Harry Wright's fifth championship, it was clearly tainted by the crooked work of the "Louisville Four."

At the League's winter meeting in 1877, the suspended "Louisville Crooks," as they became known, were expelled from baseball for life.

For years afterward, Devlin pleaded for reinstatement, claiming over and over again that he was a victim of circumstances.

But Hulbert turned a deaf ear to Devlin's remonstrations. He was determined to stamp out the influence of gamblers and bring about other sorely needed reforms.

9 The Opportunist

AL SPALDING WAS at the peak of his pitching career when he paced the Chicago White Stockings to the National League's first pennant in 1876.

Strangely, however, he was standing on first base when the next season opened.

Some speculated that while Spalding's specialty was the fast ball and a change of pace, he couldn't master the curve. And curve-ball pitching was rapidly coming in vogue.

Others said he had something else on his mind.

Business.

Specifically, the sporting-goods business.

Spalding first became interested in selling sporting goods and equipment while pitching for Boston. He observed that Harry and George Wright as well as Al Reach of Philadelphia were already in the field. (Like the Wrights, Reach was one of baseball's earliest professional players.)

To Spalding, starting a business in Chicago as a supplier to western sports enthusiasts seemed like a natural opportunity.

Convinced that baseball had a bright future and confident of his own ability, Spalding, then only 26, persuaded his 19-year-old brother, James Walter, to leave his job in a Rockford bank and enter into a partnership to be known as "A. G. Spalding and Brother."

With each brother putting up $400 and their mother, Harriet, and sister Mary helping out, the firm opened a sports "emporium" in Chicago in the spring of 1876.

From the start, it appears the brothers agreed that J. Walter, or Walter as he was generally known, would handle the merchandising and the running of the store, while Al would concentrate on marketing plans and promotion. (William Thayer Brown, a young Rockford banker and Spalding's brother-in-law, joined the firm a few years later to take over manufacturing, a change that added an "s" to the company's name making it A. G. Spalding and Brothers.)

One of Al's first moves was an attempt to corner the market for baseballs. It was sound strategy for this reason: Up until 1876, the home team supplied the game balls and, understandably, the home team always selected a ball that would give them an advantage. A heavy-hitting team, for example, liked a lively ball, while a weak hitting team favored a "dead" ball.

As a result, those who manufactured and supplied baseballs at the time offered balls that varied sharply in composition, even though each ball was 9¼ inches in circumference and weighed 5¼ ounces.

Shortly after A. G. Spalding and Brother opened its doors, Spalding was able to convince the League that it should adopt a uniform ball. And even though most clubs favored a well-made "dead" ball, Spalding opined that the ball should be lively enough to keep the customers awake.

Furthermore, if a ball was driven out of the park and not returned promptly, it should be replaced. Cut or scuffed balls should also be replaced.

The ball selected, of course, should be made to League specifications. If supplied by Spalding, it would carry the Spalding name.

To seal the deal and box out any competitors, Spalding offered to pay the League $1 for every dozen balls used in League play.

Since the baseball itself was such a major item of expense and so critical to the enjoyment of the game, these were powerful arguments.

In 1878, Spalding reached an agreement with the National League to supply the balls for all League games. It remained in effect for almost 100 years.

Spalding also went after authority to publish the League's "official" baseball *Guide*, which was first brought out by Al Reach in 1876.

Spalding succeeded in getting the rights for the Guide by simply paying the League for the privilege of publishing it. Presumably, he made a bid that Al Reach was unable or unwilling to match.

Of course, in all of his dealings with the League, his prestige, his involvement in League affairs and his relationship with the League President — Will Hulbert — contributed to his success.

Still, it has to be admitted that the proposals and deals he offered were well-thought-out and attractive from the League's point of view.

When Spalding moved to first base in '77, he played every game and batted .256 as the team's leadoff hitter. He also made 472 put-outs while wearing a conspicuous black glove, a product his firm would soon be the first to introduce, along with a long line of Spalding products that included a unique scorebook, the design of which is still in use.

Chicago, the defending champion, finished a poor fifth in a six-team race due, some said, to poor managing.

Spalding, of course, did indeed have business on his mind that year. And he was enough of a businessman to realize that he was wearing too many hats. It was his last year as an active player and field manager.

But, as he later demonstrated while energetically concentrating on the affairs of the White Stockings, the National League and A. G. Spalding and Brothers, he remained the classic opportunist who exemplified the motto that faced visitors from atop his desk:

"Everything is Possible To Him Who Dares".

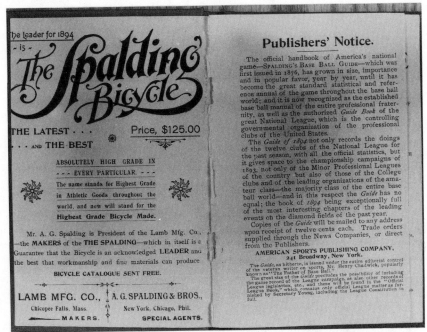

Al Spalding cornered the market on baseballs and the "official" baseball Guide. Note that Editor Henry Chadwick is identified as the "Father of Base Ball," a title attributed to at least four others.

10 Beer and Whiskey

A LTHOUGH THERE WERE bright spots, the National League came close to foundering during the first six years of its existence. Luckily for the League, it had, in Will Hulbert, a strong, intelligent, tenacious leader who worked without letup to keep the circuit afloat during this chaotic period.

When it was founded in 1876, the League set out to establish a high moral standard for baseball. Its supporters—particularly Hulbert, Harry Wright and Al Spalding—argued over and over again that baseball must be "respectable and honorable" if it were to survive.

What they wanted, they said, was an honest game; the highest caliber of play possible; a game free of alcoholic, uncontrollable players; and the elimination of rowdyism on the field or among the spectators.

Understandably, the League also wanted something even more basic: It wanted to make money.

To attain all of these objectives, the League hoped to have an exclusive circuit of eight clubs, each of which would be located in a major population area.

From everyone's point of view, these were worthy goals. And, on paper, the task seemed simple. In reality, it wasn't.

Between 1876 and 1882, the makeup of the League changed every year. And for two of those years, it operated with six clubs.

During this period, clubs representing 10 different cities entered the ranks, including Buffalo, Providence, Brooklyn, Cleveland, Detroit, Milwaukee, Troy, Worcester, Syracuse and Louisville. By '82, only two of the original eight — Chicago and Boston — were still in the League.

There were a number of reasons for this turmoil, the most important being that clubs simply couldn't meet expenses, a circumstance aggravated by a depression that gripped the country in the late 1870s.

But even after the depression passed, the turnover of franchises continued.

At the root of the League's problems was Hulbert's rigid position on three important rules:

- No Sunday ball.
- No selling of whiskey and beer in the ballparks.
- An admission price of 50¢.

Since Sunday ball was against the law in most cities and churches were opposed to it, who could say Hulbert and his friends were wrong? And serving beer and whiskey in the ballparks, the League insisted, could only lead to hooliganism and unruly crowds.

The argument about the 50¢ admission also seemed valid: 50¢ was in line with the prices charged for other forms of entertainment. Furthermore, a lowering of admission would mean a cut in player salaries, which were already too low.

While League views were applauded in Boston and Chicago, there was a rising crescendo of scorn and repudiation elsewhere, particularly in Cincinnati, St. Louis, New York and Philadelphia.

All among this group were out of the League but Cincinnati by 1879 because, in one way or another, they had broken the League's code of conduct.

Fed up with what they considered Hulbert's "pious" attitude, Cincinnati ignored the ban on the selling of beer in the ballparks and the rule on Sunday ball. As expected, Hulbert cracked down during the winter meeting of 1880 and Cincinnati was axed.

Although Hulbert had scores of supporters, the attitude of the League—perceived as being haughty, autocratic and unforgiving—alienated many.

By refusing to put a club in New York and Philadelphia, by refusing to consider Sunday ball or to relax the rule against beer and whiskey in the parks, and by ruthlessly expelling clubs and players, the League virtually invited competition.

Still, competition developed in a casual manner. It began when Alfred H. Spink, a St. Louis sportswriter, organized a team under the name used by the original St. Louis member of the National League—the Browns (nee, the Brown Stockings).

Spink persuaded Chris Von der Ahe, the owner of a delicatessen, bar, boarding house and amusement park, to back the team. He then wrote to another sportswriter—Oliver Perry Caylor of Cincinnati—presumably because he was aware of the fact that Caylor was the author of several scathing attacks on "Boss Hulbert."

In his letter, he suggested to Caylor that he, too, organize a team, name it the "Reds" after Harry Wright's famous 1869 club and bring it to St. Louis for a weekend series during the summer of 1881.

The Reds, it was proposed, would be guaranteed expenses and a share of the gate receipts.

Caylor accepted the challenge, and when the two teams met they were greeted by a large Sunday crowd. Admission was 25¢ and Von der Ahe served food and beer. Everyone, it seems, had a good time and—most importantly—both clubs made money.

That summer, other teams were invited to St. Louis and the results were the same.

Inevitably, a new league sprang into being over the winter of 1881–82. Called the American Association, it was headed by H. D. McKnight of Pittsburgh and included six clubs—Baltimore, St. Louis, Cincinnati, Pittsburgh, Louisville and Philadelphia.

The legislation that governed the Association was patterned after that of the National League with obvious exceptions—the price of admission was to be set by the home team (usually 25¢), Sunday games were allowed, and so was the selling of beer and whiskey.

Since the principal backers of four of the clubs owned breweries, the American Association became known as the "beer and whiskey" circuit. When it was born, it touched off player raids by both sides.

But the advocates of beer and whiskey were not to be denied.

11 Forgotten

WITH THE APPROACH of spring in 1882, the National League members were called to a special meeting in Chicago to discuss how they might cope with the threat posed by the newly formed American Association.

When the meeting got underway on a blustery March day, the League's guiding light and strongman, Will Hulbert, was absent. It was reported that he was seriously ill.

A month later, Hulbert died, the result of what was described as "the complications of heart disease and dropsy." He was 49.

While Hulbert's passing came as a shock to the world of baseball it also, for a brief period at least, prompted those who knew him, or of him, to reflect on his contribution to what was already being referred to as "America's national pastime."

Players, owners, editorial writers, sportswriters and fans were virtually unanimous in the view that Hulbert deserved all the credit for establishing the National League.

The day after his death, for example, the White Stockings' stockholders and players met at the club's offices. W. I. Culver, a prominent Chicago lawyer, addressed the group and had this to say:

"He was an originator, not an adapter of ideas. This is exemplified by the work he left behind, for it will be admitted without question that the League legislation was his creation, and its perfection of plan and detail and the excellent results it has already accomplished prove the foresight and comprehensiveness of mind of its originator."

Later, the stockholders passed a resolution which said in part that to Hulbert "almost alone is due the present standard of right and honorable dealing so vigorously enforced by the National League . . . "

It went on to point out that it was Hulbert "who conceived the idea of the League itself and to him more than any other are due the main features of League legislation and discipline."

These sentiments were also echoed in a resolution unanimously adopted by the League, which read in part ". . . to him alone is due the credit of having founded the League and to his able leadership, sound judgment and impartial management are chiefly due the success it has so far achieved."

The Chicago Tribune noted that Hulbert "was rightly considered to be the brains and backbone" of the National League.

The Tribune added, "In him, the game of baseball had the most useful friend and protector it has ever had; and in his death this popular pastime suffers a loss the importance of which cannot be easily exaggerated. There is not in America a player, club officer or patron of the game who will not feel that the loss is irreparable."

In Cincinnati, where Hulbert's rulings against the local team had stirred up considerable animosity, the *Enquirer* conceded that "no man had done as much to elevate and foster the game as had he."

It went on to point out that the League's "wise legislation, strong system of discipline and commendable rules" were all due to Hulbert's "wonderful mental abilities."

"His whole soul," the paper added, "was wrapped up in the organization of which he had been the prime organizer, and he studied week in and week out the best ideas to further enhance the attractiveness of the sport, and make it pure and unalloyed."

Spalding's Baseball Guide, while hardly an independent voice, said Hulbert "above all other men" should be given credit for "rescuing the game from the evils into which it had fallen and from the ruin into which it was drifting. . . ."

Such tributes—and there were many more—were unusual for any individual and unprecedented for a baseball figure, especially one who was not a player.

But for those seriously interested in the origin and development of Major League baseball, the key question is this: How close to the truth were the accolades heaped on Hulbert after his sudden death?

The record speaks for itself. It shows clearly that Hulbert:

- Originated the idea of establishing a league of professional clubs (as contrasted to the old players' league).
- With the advice and assistance of others, he founded and established the National League.
- Devoted almost all of his time for the next six years to the extremely burdensome and difficult task of holding the League together while forcing its members and players to live up to the rules.
- Lived long enough to see the League stabilized and show its first profits.

It's true, of course, that Hulbert and other prominent members of the National League underestimated the tastes and desires of thousands of baseball's patrons, a failure of perception that opened the door to competition from the American Association. But it's also true that the rival League recognized the value of Hulbert's work by adopting virtually all of the National's rules and regulations.

Not surprisingly, the knee-jerk remembrances of Hulbert and what he meant to baseball were quickly forgotten after his death.

What is surprising, however, is that Morgan Bulkeley was the first among the pioneers and officials of the National League to be voted into the Hall of Fame after it was established in 1936.

Bulkeley, who held the post only nine months, became a mayor of Hartford, Connecticut and a U.S. Senator from that state. He contributed virtually nothing to baseball.

In 1973, the Society of American Baseball Research suggested that "chances are increasing" that Hulbert would be enshrined in the Hall during the 1976 centennial of the National League.

"Appropriate recognition" of Hulbert, the Association said, "is about 35 years overdue."

At this writing, it is still overdue.

While Hulbert (who is eligible for election by the Veterans Committee as contrasted to the Players Committee) has been "considered," he has yet to enter the hallowed portals of the shrine at Cooperstown.

In other words, his critical contribution to the success of the Major Leagues has been forgotten.

12 The Fourth Step

ABRAHAM GILBERT MILLS was the least known and least appreciated of baseball's founding fathers.

Although he was once identified as the "Bismarck of Baseball," it would be more appropriate to liken him to Thomas Jefferson or James Madison, for Mills conceived and wrote the basic body of legislation that holds professional baseball together to this day.

Mills was elected unanimously as the third President of the National League during the winter meetings of 1881–82. As such, he was called on to cope with the crisis created by the death of William Hulbert and the simultaneous outbreak of baseball's first interleague "war."

The League could not have made a better choice. The 38-year-old Mills was fearless, hard-working, intelligent and a man of great integrity.

Like Hulbert, Al Spalding and Harry Wright, Mills had a broad view of baseball as a business enterprise.

Unlike the others, however, he was a lawyer with a keen legal mind. When he looked at baseball and all of its problems, he thought in terms of written agreements and contracts as a way of bringing order out of disorder.

Born and raised in New York City, he studied law at George Washington Law School and was admitted to the bar in Washington, D.C.

A Colonel in the Union Army during the Civil War, Mills was so enamored of baseball that he carried a ball and bat to Army encampments along with his side arms.

Following the War, Mills became President of the Washington Olympics and played with that team in the National Players Association.

While living in Chicago several years later, Mills wrote a newspaper article sharply critical of National League clubs for stealing players under contract to small, local teams. In the article, he outlined a plan to protect the local clubs, but make players available to the National in an orderly and responsible manner.

Hulbert was so impressed with the article that he asked Mills to detail his ideas on paper so he could circulate them among League members. The result was a written agreement that became known as the "League Alliance."

The agreement stipulated that for a fee of $10, professional Minor League clubs could join the Alliance and be bound by the same rules and regulations that applied to the National League, particularly with respect to territorial rights and player control.

From then until Hulbert's death, Mills acted as an advisor to the League on legal and other matters.

When he took over the National League, his first priority, obviously, was to hold the League together and win the battle with the upstart American Association.

Abraham Mills, third President of the National League, played a key role in establishing Organized Baseball but has yet to even be "considered" for election to the Hall of Fame.

Following the 1882 season, when Troy and Worcester obligingly resigned from the League, Mills seized the opportunity to move back into two of the nation's largest cities, Philadelphia and New York.

By granting a franchise to John B. Day in New York and Al Reach in Philadelphia, he put the League back on an even footing with the Association in terms of potential audience. While Day, the head of an entertainment company, already owned the New York Metropolitans, he chose to organize a new team for the League entry. (Eventually, the two new teams became known as the New York Giants and the Philadelphia Phillies.)

The Association countered by granting a franchise to Day's Metropolitans. It then added Columbus; now both loops consisted of eight teams.

While the Association let it be known that it was ready to sign any League player, Mills warned his troops that a switch in loyalty would mean heavy fines and suspensions.

To make players available to New York and Philadelphia and keep them out of the clutches of the Association, Mills reinstated all suspended players but the "Louisville Four."

Among those returned to the fold were a few contract jumpers and 10 "lushers" barred by Hulbert the previous season.

While good pennant races in both circuits increased attendance, the jumping of players from one loop to the other escalated salaries rapidly, just as free agency would do more than 100 years later.

The big difference, of course, was that television and the enormous revenue it produces for baseball didn't exist in the 1880s; baseball relied solely on gate receipts to cover expenses, the largest item of which was player salaries.

It became obvious to Mills that a way had to be found to stabilize the movement of players or professional baseball would surely collapse.

Expanding on the idea embraced by the League Alliance, Mills proposed an agreement that would bind all baseball organizations and clubs together wherever they were located; an agreement that would allow each league or association to run its affairs as it saw fit, but still conform to certain fundamental rules.

Essentially, these rules would:

- Control the movement of players (the reserve rule).
- Establish territorial rights.
- Require all clubs to honor each other's contracts.
- Require each club to bar players who were suspended or expelled.
- Guarantee a reserved player in the Majors a minimum salary of $1,000 and $750 in the Minors.
- Establish a procedure for settling disputes.

At first, Mills' overtures got a cool reception from the American Association. By coincidence, however, a group of backers was attempting to organize eight towns in the Midwest into a revived Northwestern League.

Mills convinced the Association that the three parties should get together for their mutual benefit on February 17, 1883, in New York.

After the so-called "harmony meeting" ended, the three groups signed the "Tripartite Agreement" (later known as the National Agreement). When they did so, baseball moved through the fourth important step in its evolutionary process, a step preceded by (a) formation of the first all-professional team; (b) the origin of the first all-professional League; and (c) the founding of the National League.

The result of Mills' efforts became known as Organized Baseball, an entity that still exists.

13 Slavery or Salvation?

T HE HEART OF the basic legislation Abraham Mills fashioned to put all of professional baseball under one regulatory umbrella was the reserve rule.

This much disputed innovation was introduced by the National league in 1879 when each League club secretly "reserved" five players.

Each club, in other words, listed five players who were not up for grabs during the year or at year's end.

If a reserved player were suspended, or quit his team, he would be blackballed and every club in the League was pledged not to hire him.

The original National Agreement written by Mills stipulated that each club could now reserve 11 players, or, in those days, the entire team.

While Mills' rules and regulations were applauded by most of the owners, they did not sit well with the players, who complained that the reserve rule made them nothing more than "slaves."

Among those who sympathized with the players was a wealthy young St. Louisian named Henry V. Lucas. Heir to a railroad fortune, Lucas had been an amateur player and the manager of an amateur team in St. Louis.

In the fall of '83, he organized the "Union Association of Base Ball Clubs." This new league adopted all the rules that governed the National League and American Association except the reserve rule.

By excluding the reserve, Lucas reasoned that he would have no difficulty attracting the stars of the two Majors to fill the rosters of Union Association teams.

Fed by Lucas' fortune, the "Onions," as they were dubbed, began by establishing franchises in eight towns—Altoona (Pennsylvania), Baltimore, Boston, Chicago, Cincinnati, Philadelphia, Washington and St. Louis.

The lure of more money, the promise of freedom from the reserve lists, or a combination of both prompted some of the biggest stars of the game to jump their contracts and join the Unions in 1884.

While there were some great individual and team performances that year, the season proved a disaster for all—fans, players, the three Major Leagues and the Minors.

The basic problem: too many teams (34) and not enough patrons to support them.

Hardest hit was the neophyte Union Association. In an effort to maintain an eight-team schedule, the Unions fielded 13 teams. One lasted a month, one only a week. By the time the season ended, only two remained and the "Onions" were dead.

The National League and the American Association were also hurt badly; the Association dropping four expansion teams and the National losing the Cleveland franchise after the season ended.

In the meantime, half a dozen minor loops folded.

Through it all, Abraham Mills fought a relentless battle to hold things together. Day in and day out during the long spring and summer months, he cajoled, threatened, bluffed and schemed to keep individual members of the National Agreement alive and the nine Major and Minor circuits intact.

Early in the season, for instance, the Unions staged a raid on the National League Cleveland club and successfully signed three of its best players. The Cleveland owners termed the loss of the trio "a death blow" and appeared ready to throw in the towel.

Mills, however, hurriedly worked out a plan to supply Cleveland with new players and subsidize gate losses so Cleveland could stay in the race.

A short time later, Providence began to waver when Charles Sweeney, the first man in baseball history to strike out 19 batters, jumped to the St. Louis Maroons, the Union club owned by Henry Lucas.

Mills promptly contacted the owners and, in strong, persuasive language, urged them to hang on. Fortunately, they did.

Mills' problems, however, were not limited to the incursions of the Union Association. His own members gave him headaches too.

Charles Sweeney, shown here on one of
the earliest baseball cards, jumped from
the National League Providence club to
the "Onions" after becoming the first
pitcher to strike out 19 batters.

During the fracas, as a case in point, Mills had a run-in with his old
friend and supporter, Al Spalding, over what he considered the im-
proper actions of a Spalding employee, Samuel Morton. Morton, a clerk
in Spalding's Chicago store, operated an employment agency that special-
ized in locating players for ballclubs. The Unions were among his
clients.

When Mills discovered this, he said he would give Spalding "a piece
of my mind" and put a stop to Morton's activities "or go out of baseball."

He won that point, but Mills then had to struggle with others in the
League and Association who wanted to drop the Northwestern League
(a minor league) because some clubs allegedly failed to pay the players.

Mills, however, insisted on keeping the Northwestern loop alive so
the players wouldn't be free to switch to the Unions. Northwestern's
losses, however, were too much to overcome.

The single-season war with the "Onions" was the first battle between
those who saw the reserve rule and the National Agreement as a means
of survival and those who were convinced that the interlocking legislation was nothing more than a new form of slavery.

Although the Unions were beaten decisively, the issue would surface
again and again in the years to follow.

14 Ignored

WITH THE END of the Union Association war, Abraham Mills faced the difficult task of putting Organized Baseball back together on a workable and profitable footing.

Almost immediately, however, an internal political battle erupted over several thorny issues. The most serious involved Henry Lucas and the players who had broken their contracts to join the Union Association. Having lost the war, Lucas was determined to keep his Maroons in the Majors and quickly made overtures to the National League.

Surprisingly, he received a warm response from Al Spalding and a few others who argued that replacing the shattered Cleveland club with the strong St. Louis Maroons (winners of the Union Association pennant by a wide margin) would be a boon to the League.

There were four sticky problems that would have to be worked out if a deal was to be struck, however. They included:

1. The players Lucas pirated from Cleveland: Lucas wanted to keep them.
2. Lucas' attitude toward the reserve rule: To be accepted by the National League, he would have to recant.
3. Chris Von der Ahe, owner of the Association's St. Louis Browns: He was dead set against competing with a team (the Maroons) that had already cost him and the League a lot of money.
4. Abraham Mills, the League President: To him, the National Agreement amounted to baseball law and violators should be punished. In other words, he was opposed to accommodating Lucas and reinstating any of the 27 key players who had broken their contracts. (He recommended that contract jumpers be fined $500 each; reserved jumpers $1,000. All, he said, should also be suspended "so they understand the enormity of their offense.")

By the windup of the League meetings that November, the Spalding clique resolved all of these matters as follows:

- The players would be reinstated if they paid a fine for their transgressions.
- With the players reinstated, Lucas would agree publicly that the reserve rule was a practical necessity.
- To appease Von der Ahe, the League promised that the Browns would be the only team in St. Louis allowed to play Sunday ball, sell beer and keep the price of admission at 25¢ (as contrasted to 50 in the National).

- As to Mills, who saw giving in to the players as a show of "supine weakness," that was the simplest item of all to resolve: the League accepted his resignation and elected Nick Young in his place.

It was all a matter of business, you see.

To offset the shabby treatment of Mills, however, the National League members gave him the title of "Honorary President" — a gesture he spurned not long afterward.

H. D. McKnight, President of the American Association, was one of several who regretted Mills' decision to resign.

"I am indeed sorry that you are determined to abandon us, but I suppose your decision is final," McKnight said in a letter to Mills after his resignation that fall. "The American Association owes you almost as much gratitude as the League for your past services, making peace between the two associations and inventing the National Agreement."

By creating the legislation for Organized Baseball and piloting the National League through two devastating "wars" (without pay, by the way), Mills had made a significant contribution to baseball.

Despite their differences during this tumultuous period, Spalding and Mills remained friends for life. Over the years, Mills also maintained his contacts with baseball and occasionally was called on for advice and assistance.

Mills, for many years a Senior Vice President of the Otis Elevator Company, had a lifelong interest in athletics. He once was a Director and President of the New York Athletic Club; and in 1921 he suggested organizing the American Olympic Association, and drew up its constitution.

At the time of his death on August 26, 1929 (he was 85), Mills was President of the Association for the Protection of the Adirondacks and involved in making plans for the Winter Olympics at Lake Placid in 1932.

Spalding, who died long before Mills, said in his memoirs, "Most fortunate indeed, was the National League that, when William A. Hulbert was suddenly removed by death . . . one so eminently qualified as A. G. Mills was found to take his place. It needed just such a man to carry out the work of the League so ably begun. . . A lawyer of splendid ability, as immediately demonstrated by the formulation of the National Agreement, a document that has stood the ravages of time and the wearing warfare of the courts; and an executive of sterling endowments in the way of administering affairs and managing men. . . ."

The 1926 *Spalding Guide* noted that, with the exception of Hulbert, Mills was "the most forceful of the earlier Presidents of the National League."

"Hulbert was an organizer and a disciplinarian of players," the *Guide* said. "Mills was a perpetuator, an advocate of unwavering honesty between clubs and leagues and even more of a builder for the future than Hulbert."

It added that while Hulbert made the National League possible, it was Mills who made Organized Baseball possible.

While *The Sporting News* expressed similar sentiments, it added, "The enforcement of the National Agreement made the question of territory and players inviolate. Without it each year would have found the wealthier clubs driving the less fortunate out of the game by easy stages of tyranny. . . .

"To Colonel Mills, there was an atmosphere of honor about baseball that must include everything to the smallest detail. Honesty of course was imperative, but he wanted more than that. He wished the game to represent in an athletic way the life of the nation."

Years after the war with the Union Association, Mills, at Spalding's request, put together a document that declared baseball was originated by Abner Doubleday at Cooperstown, New York.

That document led to the establishment of The National Baseball Hall of Fame and Museum.

Ironically, like Hulbert, the third founding father of the Major Leagues, Mills has also been omitted from the Hall. Unlike Hulbert, he has never been considered even though, on at least one occasion, the Veterans Committee failed to come up with a suitable candidate for election.

15 The Adversary

WHILE THE NATIONAL AGREEMENT represented a tremendous step forward in the development of Major League baseball, Abraham Mills' historic document contained the most disputed condition the game has ever known.

It was, of course, the reserve rule, which was later written into player contracts and became known as the "reserve clause."

In the context of the National Agreement, this rule was often deemed unfair because it failed to give players appropriate rights as employees.

Initially, baseball law gave the owners the right to:

- Sell a player without his consent.
- Sell a player without giving him a share of the sales price.
- Terminate a contract with 10 days' notice.
- Bind a player to a club from one year to the next by application of the reserve rule.

If a player balked at the salary an owner offered and refused to sign a contract, he could be blacklisted. Under terms of the National Agreement, no other club was permitted to hire him.

Unlike the owner, a player did not have the right or freedom to terminate a contract. The only escape was to quit baseball.

In fairness, as Mills clearly understood, a strict code of conduct was badly needed to enable baseball to survive the early (and later) years.

Many of the ballplayers, for example, were illiterate alcoholics. By the same token, many of the owners were unscrupulous charlatans whose only interest in baseball was to make an easy dollar.

The purpose of the National Agreement was to stabilize the game, keep it honest and rid it of undesirable elements; to establish conditions, in other words, that would benefit all—players, magnates and fans.

While Mills did not intend that the National Agreement should be abused, many of the owners couldn't resist using the power it gave them to the utmost.

Charlie Jones, the popular Cincinnati outfielder Will Hulbert signed and returned in 1877, is a case in point.

Jones moved to Boston in 1879, batted .355 and led the League in runs scored and runs batted in.

In June of the following year, he distinguished himself by becoming the first player to hit two homers in one inning.

When Boston failed to give him $378 in back pay after the first several weeks of the '81 season, he also distinguished himself by refusing to play.

Owner Arthur Soden's response was to suspend Jones while the team was on the road and fine him $100.

Jones didn't play in the Majors again until he joined the Cincinnati club of the American Association in 1883, two years later.

Soden also suspended and fined Stephen "Sadie" Houck because the outfielder didn't tip his hat when they passed on the street.

In another instance, the Washington club fined a player $100 because he was late to the park on his wedding day.

The owners were also known to have ballplayers cut the infield and outfield grass, handle tickets and clean up the seats and stands.

Small wonder, then, that this kind of treatment aroused the ire of not only the players, but of the public and several sportswriters.

While individual players took owners to court on several occasions, the first serious effort to organize as a group took place in 1885, when a sportswriter named Bill Voltz founded the National Brotherhood of Professional Baseball Players.

At the time, there appeared to be no thought of taking any sort of concerted action against the owners. But that winter, the owners decided to put a ceiling of $2,000 on player salaries. Worst of all, they agreed not to advance any money against a player's pay. This was a hardship for many, since few ballplayers were equipped to earn a living in the offseason.

This typically arbitrary action by the owners suddenly brought the Brotherhood to life. To lead them, the players elected a new president, John Montgomery Ward, the 26-year-old Captain and shortstop of the New York Giants.

Ward had a brilliant career as a pitcher for Providence from 1878 to 1882. In 1879, for example, Ward won 47 games as Providence captured the pennant under manager George Wright.

The next year, he became the second pitcher to hurl a perfect game when he beat Buffalo 5 to o. (John Lee Richmond pitched the first perfect game just five days earlier as Worcester defeated Cleveland 1 to o.)

Ward was a fine athlete and a serious student of the game. When he hurt his arm after being traded to the Giants, he learned to play the

John Montgomery Ward, champion of players' rights.

outfield and second base, but switched to shortstop to 1884, a position he played to the end of his career.

John Ward was not your average run-of-the-mill ballplayer. A graduate of Penn State, he went to Columbia University while playing for the Giants and earned degrees in law and political science. He also married a glamorous Broadway actress, Helen Dauvray, and the two were familiar figures in New York cafe society.

Above and beyond that, Ward was a man of integrity and a fighter. As time would tell, the owners had their first and most important adversary in John Montgomery Ward. As such, he would establish a pattern for major changes in professional baseball.

16 A Failed Promise

B ECAUSE THE OWNERS had such extraordinary power over the lives of the players, John Ward moved cautiously as he began to build the Brotherhood into a viable organization.

He recognized from the outset that the Brotherhood had to strike a posture that would appeal to three groups:

- The public.
- The press.
- The few honest owners and managers—such as Al Spalding and Harry Wright, for example—then in control of baseball.

He began by secretly establishing Brotherhood chapters among the League and Association clubs. Not every player was welcome to join, however. Ward recognized that if baseball were to prosper, the game must rid itself of drunks, hooligans and gamblers. As a result, the Brotherhood constitution spelled out its major objectives with these words, "To protect and benefit ourselves collectively and individually. To promote a high standard of professional conduct. To foster and encourage the interests of Base Ball. . . ."

The owners were either unaware of what was going on or didn't care, for they were silent on the subject of the Brotherhood until late in 1885. By then, Ward and his colleagues had recruited more than 100 members.

Ward then began a campaign to win the support of sportswriters, and through them the general public. While he was not entirely successful, several influential publications published his letters and articles.

His theme was consistent:

- He recognized that the reserve rule gave the game stability, and stability was good for all concerned.
- He abhorred the buying, selling and trading of players without their consent or profit.
- He was opposed to any rule that would tie a player to a club for life.
- He was opposed to using the reserve rule as a weapon to reduce salaries.

Ward's arguments got their biggest boost when Al Spalding sold Michael J. "King" Kelly to Boston in the spring of 1887 for the then-staggering sum of $10,000.

Kelly, who caught and played the infield and outfield, had joined Chicago in 1884 after two years with Cincinnati. At his peak, he was truly "King of the Diamond," probably the best all-around player of his day. It was he who developed the hook slide, which in turn inspired the phrase "Slide, Kelly! Slide!" He delighted fans with his antics both on and off the diamond.

A handsome, dark-haired Irishman who believed in living life to the fullest, Kelly had a fondness for liquor, ladies and late hours.

Convinced that Kelly's behavior set a bad example for the younger Chicago players, Spalding, with Cap Anson's concurrence, decided to get rid of him after the 1886 season — even though he led the League in hitting with a .388 average as the White Stockings won the pennant.

The sale of "The $10,000 Beauty," as Kelly became known, made ballplayers suddenly realize that their contracts had considerable value.

The Kelly transaction also created more publicity than baseball had ever before experienced.

Ward took advantage of the uproar by writing a scathing article about the injustice of baseball contracts for *Lippincott's Magazine*, titled "Is The Base-Ball Player A Chattel?"

He pointed out that in establishing the reserve rule the owners were probably motivated by three things, " . . . they wished to make the business of base-ball more permanent, they meant to reduce salaries and they sought to secure a monopoly of the game. . . ."

He said baseball contracts provided "no escape" for players and likened it to "a fugitive-slave law." He then raised a key question about the rights of players, citing Kelly as an example, "What did the Chicago club ever give Kelly in return for the right to control his future services?"

In addition to his writing campaign, Ward launched a frontal attack on the owners, asking them directly to recognize the Brotherhood. At first the owners, through President Nick Young of the National League, ignored Ward. But finally, at Spalding's urging, the League appointed a committee to meet with a Brotherhood group that included Ward, Dennis Brouthers and Ned Hanlon.

When the two groups got together, Ward's committee complained about the reserve rule. The owners' committee said, in effect, "show us a better way to run the game."

Ward was unable to give an immediate response, but later the Brotherhood offered what it termed a "model contract." In effect, it would: put the reserve rule into individual contracts; eliminate the $2,000 ceiling on salaries and spell out salaries in contracts; and prohibit a reduction of salaries.

The Brotherhood also agreed that players ought to be disciplined for drunkenness and general misconduct, but insisted that fines and suspensions should be applied evenly.

While Ward did succeed in getting agreement on several items, the League refused to eliminate the salary ceiling, the Brotherhood's major objective.

Young said the League couldn't accede to this demand without the concurrence of the American Association. He promised to review the issue when the two leagues met in the spring of 1888.

The promise was never kept; a failure all of baseball would live to regret.

As "King of the Diamond," Mike Kelly inspired the phrase "Slide Kelly! Slide!"

17 The Last Straw

WHEN JOHN WARD accepted appointment as Captain of the New York Giants, he did so only after being assured he would be in full charge of the team on the diamond.

Ward didn't disappoint the owners or the Giant fans.

With Tim Keefe (his brother-in-law) leading the League's pitchers with a 33–11 record, the 1888 Giants breezed to their first National League pennant, nine lengths ahead of Al Spalding's powerful Chicago White Stockings.

What's more, the Giants went on to conquer the St. Louis Browns in the World Series. The Browns, managed by young Charles Comiskey, had won the Association championship three years running.

Adding to the excitement of the pennant races and post-season games was an announcement by the inimitable Al Spalding that he planned to take his White Stockings and a team of "All Americans" on an exhibition tour overseas. This time, he said, he would cross the Pacific instead of the Atlantic (as he had in 1874).

Spalding's original destination was Australia, but the trip soon expanded to a "world tour."

In an era when it was a novelty to travel across one's own state, the proposed barnstorming venture captured the imagination of fans and sportswriters everywhere.

And while the tour would be the biggest promotional event baseball had ever witnessed, it also fit in with Spalding's plans to expand the market for the products sold by A. G. Spalding and Brothers.

These products, featured by 1,000 illustrations in the Spalding catalog, not only included a full line of baseball equipment and uniforms, but ranged from fishing tackle to gym equipment and bicycles.

After a reception by President Grover Cleveland at the White House, Spalding's players, led by Adrian Anson, and the All Americans, managed by John Ward, officially opened the tour with a game in Chicago. Appropriately enough, Spalding pitched the first few innings.

Traveling west from Chicago, the teams played 18 more exhibition games in Denver, Omaha, Los Angeles and other cities before thousands of fans, most of whom had never seen Major League baseball.

When the entourage of 35 sailed from San Francisco, it included, in addition to the players, three newsmen, umpire George Wright, Spalding's mother, Harriet, the White Stockings' black mascot, Clarence Duval, and several players' wives.

After a stop in Hawaii, the group traveled to Australia and then to

On a "world tour" sponsored by Al Spalding, ballplayers pose with the Sphinx in Egypt.

Ceylon, Egypt, Italy, France, England, Scotland and Ireland. In all, the exhibitions drew some 200,000 spectators, including the King and Queen of Italy and the Prince of Wales.

While John Ward and several of the game's top players were making that astonishing six-month journey, however, trouble aplenty was brewing at home.

John T. Brush, President of the Indianapolis club, had persuaded the other club owners to adopt a new, more restrictive salary plan for 1889.

Instead of the $2,000 ceiling imposed on the players during the previous season, the plan established a "classification" for each player, based on behavior, dependability and skill.

In other words, the players were arbitrarily assigned a Class A, B, C, D or E contract. Salaries ranged from $2,500 for the so-called "A" players to $1,500 for those identified as "E" players.

With the President of the Brotherhood and the others away, there was little those back home could do but sign for the season.

All of this was made known to Spalding and Ward when their ship, the Adriatic, sailed into New York harbor three days late at dawn of April 6.

When all had landed, the players gathered in a knot around Ward on the pier, while the owners conferred with Spalding.

Having digested the news about the Brush plan, Ward promptly approached Spalding.

He said he wanted to discuss the salary matter immediately.

"John," Spalding was reported to have said, "there's nothing to discuss."

In the weeks that followed, various members of the Brotherhood began to pressure Ward to do something about the owners' "treachery."

Ward pointed out that little could be done since almost all players were under contract for '89 and the season was about to get underway.

After cooling off the hotheads, Ward made another effort to resolve matters by asking for a meeting between representatives of the National League—the stronger and more important of the two leagues—and the Brotherhood. At first, the League agreed. But once the season opened, it pointedly forgot about the meeting.

For John Ward, that was the last straw.

18 Revolt

T O THE OUTSIDER in the spring of 1889, it looked as though the members of the Brotherhood had lost their brief battle over "Classification" with the men who ran Organized Baseball.

That June, however, John Ward unveiled a daring plan: All Brotherhood members would leave their clubs after the season and join new teams in a "Players League," which would be formed by the spring of 1890.

To succeed, Ward warned, the players would have to remain silent until all the "money men" needed could be found and brought into the scheme.

That summer, ironically, Washington offered the Giants $12,000 for Ward. This was $2,000 more than the record price Boston paid Spalding for the mighty King Kelly.

But Ward dumbfounded the owners by refusing to leave New York. Not willing to challenge Ward in court, the Washington and New York clubs cancelled the deal.

For New York fans, it was a happy turn of events since Ward managed the Giants to their second straight pennant and performed well on the field while doing so, batting .299 and stealing 66 bases, fourth highest in the League.

In post-season play, Ward and his Giants whipped Brooklyn, winners for the first time of the American Association Championship.

Inevitably, rumors of the impending strike began to reach the ears of the magnates of both leagues by the end of the summer.

While many scoffed at such a possibility, Spalding, ever the realist, was alarmed and pushed for a meeting with Ward in an attempt to resume the negotiations that had been broken off in the spring.

Ward had a ready response, "Remember, Al, there's nothing to discuss."

Despite threats by the owners that they would destroy the Brotherhood and punish its leaders if there were a strike, Ward scheduled an open meeting in Manhattan's Fifth Avenue Hotel for November 4, 1889 to reveal his plans.

Before the meeting, the corridors and public rooms of the famous hotel were filled with fans, newsmen and joking, back-slapping players.

From all accounts, the players hardly looked the part of poor and exploited employees of the Major Leagues. Smoking expensive cigars, they were dressed in top hats, spats, ascots and fur-lined gloves. Several twirled or carried silver-headed walking sticks.

The gathering included, according to one newspaper, "baseball enthusiasts of all calibres, from the high and mighty to the small boy whose ambition it is to carry the bat of some big hitter."

Aside from Ward, the center of attraction was King Kelly, who wore a tight-fitting pair of imported trousers, tall silk hat, beaver coat, patent leather shoes and a bright-red boutonniere in the lapel of his coat.

Just before the meeting was called to order in the hotel ballroom, Kelly spotted a "spy" near the door. It was George Billings, the young son of one of Boston's three owners, and as such one of Kelly's bosses.

To the delight of the players around him, Kelly grasped the boy by the shoulder and said, "Well, sonny, tell Pop I'm sorry for him. If he wants a job next season, I'll put him to work on one of my turnstiles. You see, I'm one of the bosses now. Next year, Presidents will have to drive horse cars for a living and borrow rain checks to see a game."

Once the meeting got under way, business was conducted in a quiet and orderly manner as, according to the *New York Times*, "Ward presided with the grace that characterized his work in the short field."

Tim Keefe, the Giants' leading pitcher, acted as Secretary and "threw ink with as much skill and proficiency as he curves an out-shoot."

Although the players were in a jocular, festive mood that day, Ward issued a statement that blistered the owners and spelled out the players' grievances.

"There was a time when the League stood for integrity and fair dealing," Ward said. "Today, it stands for dollars and cents.

"Once it looked to the elevation of the game and an honest exhibition of the sport; today its eyes are upon the turnstiles. Men have come into the business for no other motive than to exploit it for every dollar in sight. Measures originally intended for the good of the game have been

Tim Keefe, Secretary of the Brotherhood of Professional Base Ball Players and star pitcher for the Giants.

converted into instruments for wrong. The reserve rule and the provisions of the National Agreement gave the Majors unlimited power and they have not hesitated to use this in the most arbitrary and mercenary way.

"Players have been bought, sold and exchanged as though they were sheep instead of American citizens."

Ward noted that the combined magnates were "stronger than the strongest trust" and were able to enforce "the most arbitrary measures and the player has either to submit or get out of the profession."

Even when a club disbanded, Ward added, the players could not escape "the octopus clutch" and were "peddled around to the highest bidder."

Two days later, the Brotherhood representatives met with their backers and worked out a series of rules and agreements that would govern the new League. Among them were these:

- There would be no reserve or classification rule, but players would be controlled by a 16-member board.
- The players would receive the same salaries for 1890 as they earned in 1889.
- Contracts would be for three years.
- Players would share in the profits and could buy stock in their clubs.
- Visiting teams would receive half the gate receipts, but home teams would keep the profits from concessions.

- Player representatives from each club would join the owners in operating the League.
- The pitching distance was lengthened from 50 to 51 feet.
- Two umpires instead of one would govern games, and they would be dressed in white (presumably to reflect purity).

With the clarion call of the "manifesto" issued in November and the adoption of the rules and regulations less than a month later, the first and only full-season player revolt in Major League history had begun.

19 "A War To The Death"

R EACTING QUICKLY TO the announced defection of its players, the National League appointed a three-man "War Committee" to conduct its battle for survival with the Brotherhood.

The chairman of the Committee, as might be expected, was Al Spalding. The other members included John B. Day, owner of the Giants, and John I. Rogers, owner of the Philadelphia team.

With Spalding as spokesman, this trio responded to the Brotherhood charges by noting that the reserve rule came into existence in 1877 because clubs in the smaller cities faced "almost certain financial disaster. . .as a check upon competition, the weaker clubs in the League demanded the privilege of reserving five players who would form the nucleus of a team for the ensuing season," Spalding explained. "This was the origin of the reserve rule and from its adoption may be dated the development of better financial results."

Under the reserve rule, Spalding pointed out, baseball had steadily grown in favor and the salaries of players "have more than trebled."

Furthermore, Spalding said, the Brotherhood had acknowledged the need for the reserve rule during one of its grievance meetings with the League.

Thus, the Brotherhood's use of such terms as "bondage," "slavery" and "sold like sheep" were "meaningless and absurd."

Spalding also noted that while the National League had been in existence for 14 years, only in the past five years had dividends been paid to stockholders in the eight League cities.

The dividends totaled $150,000, he said, while salaries of ballplayers amounted to 10 times that much over the same period, or $1.5-million.

As usual, sportswriters took vigorous sides in the dispute, adding considerably to the war of words. One writer, referring to Ward, crowed that "St. George has slain the dragon of oppression!"

Henry Chadwick, editor of *Spalding's Baseball Guide*, saw the strike by the players as a sinister plot for "self-aggrandizement . . . headed by one man (Ward) who was the mastermind of the whole revolution scheme. . . ."

During the winter months, the Spalding Committee dropped the hated Classification Plan and offered players more money to stay with the League. But almost every week, there were announcements of more defections to the Brotherhood.

In still another costly move, the League took several players to court in an attempt to enforce the reserve rule. Among the cases were those involving John Ward, Tim Keefe and Buck Ewing.

In each ruling, handed down by a different court, the owners lost.

In the spring of 1890, the Players League opened the season with teams in New York, Brooklyn, Boston, Philadelphia, Cleveland, Chicago, Buffalo and Pittsburgh.

Cornelius McGillicudy, Connie Mack.

The Brotherhood was now in direct competition with the National League in every city but Brooklyn. Brooklyn, however, was under franchise to the American Association, as was Philadelphia, a town that now contained three Major League teams.

Cleverly, the Brotherhood named as managers of its teams some of the biggest stars of the day. Ward, for example, managed the Brooklyn "Wonders"; Kelly the Boston "Beaneaters"; Buck Ewing, New York; Charles Comiskey, Chicago; and Ned Hanlon, Pittsburgh.

The rosters of the Brotherhood teams were filled with almost all of the older National League and American Association stars as well as several bright young prospects, including Cornelius McGillicuddy (Connie Mack) of Buffalo.

In fact, only two "names" refused to join the ranks of the Brotherhood— Cap Anson and Harry Wright. Anson reportedly stayed with Chicago because he had invested in the club.

Wright, spurning several offers from the Brotherhood, felt he owed his loyalty to the League he helped found. He also made it clear that if his players weren't with him "heart and soul," he didn't want them on his team. All but four left.

As the teams went into action, each side used a number of tactics to gain the upper hand in the battle for players and patrons. The League waited until the Brotherhood announced its schedule, for instance, and then booked games on the same day in the same town.

The head-to-head scheduling backfired as fans usually stayed away from both games.

As the battle wore on, both sides began to give out false attendance figures to prove superiority and preference.

All of this led to chaos, and disgusted fans began to ignore baseball and turn to other forms of leisure.

Toward the middle of the summer, John Day told the League he would have to throw in the sponge if he couldn't come up with $80,000 immediately.

Spalding promptly called on the owners to contribute to a fund to save the Giants. He succeeded in raising the $80,000, but most of it was his own money.

There was no question now but that the Brotherhood Revolt meant, as Spalding would later phrase it, "a war to the death."

20 An Oversight

B Y AUGUST OF 1890, with gate receipts dwindling and losses mounting, the National League decided that the only way to win the war with the Brotherhood was to regain control of their major stars.

Logically, they chose Al Spalding to launch this frontal attack on the Brotherhood, as he was still highly respected by the players and regarded "as one of the boys." Reluctantly, Spalding accepted the assignment.

The first target selected in a blatant attempt to break through the ranks of the Brotherhood was none other than King Kelly, who, next to John Ward, was the most important figure in the Brotherhood galaxy.

Spalding was urged to pay any price to grab Kelly.

As Spalding remembered it, he sent Kelly a note and invited him to his hotel.

"He came," Spalding wrote in his memoirs. "We passed the usual conventional civilities, talked about health, the weather and kindred exciting topics. . . ."

Finally, he said, he laid a $10,000 check in front of the great player. The exchange, according to Spalding, went like this:

"Mike, how would you like that check for $10,000 made out to your order."

"Would Mike Kelly like $10,000? I should smile."

Spalding then offered Kelly a three-year contract and told him he could fill in the amount himself.

Kelly was incredulous.

"What does this mean?" he asked. "Does it mean that I'm to join the League? Quit the Brotherhood? Go back on the boys?"

Spalding said that was exactly what it meant and that he would have to go to Boston that very night.

Kelly decided to take a walk and think things over. On his return, he refused the offer, saying, "I can't go back on the boys. And neither would you."

He then borrowed $500 from Spalding and left.

Toward the end of the summer, the Brotherhood scored another major victory when the American Association's Cincinnati club gave up and sold out to the Players League.

When the season ended, Kelly's Boston club had won the Players League championship, beating out Ward's Brooklyn aggregation by 6½ games.

In the National League, Brooklyn finished in front, six games ahead of Chicago, while Louisville won the American Association pennant by a 10-game margin over Columbus.

But all this was meaningless, as each of the three Leagues had suffered tremendous losses as fans turned their backs on the game.

While both sides recognized that baseball was about to enter an early grave, Ward was the first to sue for peace. He had only one demand — that the Brotherhood circuit be recognized as a Major League.

Spalding responded by inviting representatives of the Players League to a meeting in October.

On the eve of the meeting, however, Spalding shrewdly insisted on dealing only with the backers of the Players League and none of the players, including Ward.

After a series of lengthy meetings, a variety of settlements, mergers and agreements were worked out among the owners of the clubs in the three leagues.

Soon after, in a popular hangout for the Giants, a saloon called "Home Plate," Ward proposed a wry toast to the Players League: "Pass the wine around, the League is dead. Long live the League."

During the winter of 1890-91, baseball again called on Abraham Mills to write a new, broader National Agreement for Organized Baseball. When completed, it contained a number of reforms prompted by the Brotherhood Revolt.

One of the major changes put control of the game in the hands of a three-man National Board that included a representative of each party to the agreement — the National League, American Association and the Minor Western League.

At first, the owners wanted Mills to become chairman, but Mills turned it down and recommended Spalding. Spalding also declined, and the post went to Alan Thurman of the American Association.

Before the end of the next season, however, the American Association, angered by the way the Board reassigned some of the players, withdrew from the National Agreement, sparking another war.

But the Association was so weakened by the Brotherhood Revolt that it finally had to give up. Four of its teams — Baltimore, Louisville, Washington and St. Louis — were merged with the National to form a 12-team circuit for the 1892 season.

That year, the only Major League in existence played for the honor of winning the Dauvray Cup, so named in honor of John Ward's actress wife.

To the disappointment of his wife, Ward's Brooklyn team finished third and the cup went to Boston.

John Ward moved to New York and managed the Giants in 1893 and 1894, taking the team from eighth to sixth to second in the standings.

He then quit the playing field and turned to practicing law. Ironically,

The winner of the Majors post-season series in the 1890s was awarded the "Dauvray Cup," presented by the lady in this autographed picture, Helen Dauvray Ward, John Ward's actress wife. New York Public Library, Spalding Collection.

he served as chief counsel for the National League for several years.

In a final fling with baseball, he bought the Boston Braves in 1912, installed George Stallings as Manager, made a deal for Johnny Evers and uncovered and signed little Rabbit Maranville for $2,200.

Two years later, Boston became known as the "Miracle Braves" when it finished 10½ games in front of the pack after being last as late as July 19.

Selling the Braves shortly afterward, Ward returned to his law practice.

During March of 1925, only a few weeks after attending the National League's Golden Jubilee in New York, Ward went on a hunting trip in Georgia, contracted pneumonia and died. He was 65.

While Ward was a great player and key figure in baseball for most of his life, he must be recognized as the first to organize a serious movement to fight for the rights of the professional ballplayer.

He also was the first to establish the fact that a players' union had a legitimate place in baseball. That precedent, adhered to even today, has changed the economics of baseball dramatically.

In 1964, along with Tim Keefe, John Ward was elected to the Hall of Fame for his brilliant performance on the diamond as a player and manager over a period of 17 years.

Nothing was said, however, about his contribution to players' rights, a serious oversight.

21 The Model

RULE CHANGES WERE so common during the first three decades of the professional game that *Spalding's Official Base Ball Guide* opened virtually every annual issue with a review of the code.

And while all of the changes nudged diamond play closer to the game we know today, a rule written in 1893 and introduced a year later marked an important turning point in baseball history. This was the rule that lengthened the pitching distance from 50 to today's 60 feet 6 inches.

Essentially, this rule separated the "early game" from the "modern game."

Harry Wright, always consulted when major changes were to be made, agreed that it was time to move the pitchers back because too many were dominating hitters with their "cyclone" deliveries.

Wright originally thought that a move from 50 to 55 feet would be enough. To go farther back, he felt, would ruin the "scientific" game. After a lengthy debate, however, the rules committee settled on the 60-foot 6-inch distance.

Interestingly enough, the year this major change in pitching rules came about marked the end of Harry Wright's baseball career; a career that started almost 30 years earlier with the New York Knickerbockers.

Wright's position on the rule change was not the reason why he parted company with the Philadelphia Phillies after managing that club for 10 years, however. Rather, he was fired.

There was speculation that Wright's departure was the result of a salary dispute. He had received $2,000 in 1892 and 1893, and while receipts were down due to a recession in 1892, they were up considerably the next year.

The Guide, in fact, reported record attendance throughout the League and said that "the majority of clubs (had) surpluses on hand" at the close of the season.

Although the Phillies made a race of it in the early months, they finished fourth in a 12-team league, 14 games behind the first-place Boston Red Sox.

Letting a manager go for not winning had become a common practice by then, of course. But Harry Wright? Harry Wright, the man to whom all in baseball owed their livelihoods?

Wright's friends were so chagrined they pressured the League to create the post of "Chief of Umpires," a meaningless job he accepted gracefully and held for two years.

Early in the fall of 1895, Wright contracted pneumonia and was

Harry Wright, lauded as the "Father" of professional baseball and a "model" player, was quickly forgotten after his death.

hospitalized in Atlantic City. On October 3, with his family around him, he seemed to be in a coma. Suddenly, however, he sat up in bed and, in a clear voice, said "two men out," then fell back to his pillow and died. He was 65.

During his lifetime, Wright was identified by Will Hulbert, Al Spalding, Henry Chadwick and others as the "Father of Professional Baseball." It was, of course, a well-deserved title, for Harry Wright, more than any other individual, was responsible for the development of the professional player and team. In addition, he played a strong role in the creation of the Major Leagues and helped them survive four early "wars."

Four of Wright's five teams in the National Players Association won pennants. And after the National League was formed, he managed three teams over an 18-year period, won two championships and was rarely out of the first division.

His skill as a manager was never better demonstrated than when he took over the Phillies in 1884, a team that in 1883 won only 17 games and ended the season with a won-loss percentage of .173. The next two years, under Wright, the Phils moved up to fourth and then to third.

Wright was honored briefly in the spring of 1896, when all National League clubs were called on to hold a "Harry Wright Day" with proceeds from the games to go to a monument for his grave site and a memorial fund for his widow and family. Only four of the Major League clubs responded, however, and these played pre-season exhibition games with either Minor League clubs or amateur teams.

In Philadelphia, where a game between the Phillies and the Minor League Athletics produced $1,400, a newspaper noted that the receipts were to go to a memorial for "the best man in every sense of the word who was ever connected with baseball."

In Rockford, Illinois, two teams of old-timers played a rain-shortened

The 1893 Phillies, Harry Wright's last team, pose at a Revolutionary War Monument in Paoli, Pennsylvania, a Philadelphia suburb. New York Public Library, Spalding Collection.

game under the rules in force in the the 1860s. Appropriately enough, Al Spalding pitched for one of the teams and playing shortstop behind him was Harry Wright's brother, George.

In Cincinnati, a team composed of former players who made up the 1882 American Association Championship "Reds" played the National League club of that day, with the Nationals winning 7 to 3.

In all, only eight games were played to honor Wright, bringing in about $10,000, some of which covered the cost of a statue that still stands at his grave in the Philadelphia area.

Upon his death, the *Philadelphia Record* said Wright was the most widely known baseball figure in the nation.

"Associating with ballplayers since boyhood, he retained a simplicity of character and straightforwardness of purpose which made him liked by everyone," the paper said. "He was honesty personified, his word being as good as his bond."

Another newspaper said that "as a player and manager, Harry Wright's name became a household word wherever the national game was known or played and no man was held in higher esteem by the general public . . ."

The Spalding Guide added that Wright was "to every worthy young ballplayer as a father to a son, and to those of older growth who were deserving of his regard, he was the true friend and counselor."

Wright, the *Guide* said, was "a model every professional player can copy from with great gain to his individual reputation and to public esteem and popularity."

Baseball, however, seemed to forget its "model" player and manager until 1953, when Wright was elected to the Hall of Fame. Even so, his brother received that honor 16 years earlier.

22 "As Good As They Come"

WHILE 1893 WAS the end of the line for Harry Wright, it was also the first year in the Majors for John Joseph McGraw.

Born in Truxton, New York, on April 7, 1873, McGraw was the first of John McGraw and Ellen Comerfort's eight children.

McGraw senior, an Irish immigrant, was a veteran of the Civil War and a widower with a small daughter. After settling in Truxton, he took a job on the railroad and married Ellen. Their life together lasted for 12 years; then Ellen died in a diphtheria epidemic that also took the lives of two sons and two daughters.

Young McGraw didn't get along very well with his father, mostly because baseball became an early passion for him and his father considered the game to be a waste of time.

Their relationship became so strained, in fact, that young John moved in with a farm family next to the McGraw home, where he worked for room and board.

Like many boys, McGraw played sandlot and high school ball, almost always as a pitcher. Toward the end of his school years, he also pitched for the Truxton Grays, a town team.

Although he was small of frame and weighed only a little more than 100 pounds, McGraw was a good left-handed hitter and effective on the mound at this level of the game. A right-hander, he was fairly fast and could throw a curve, a rare skill at the time.

After winning a few games for Truxton, McGraw was offered $2 a game to hurl for East Homer, a town five miles away. Even though he had to walk both ways, he accepted.

McGraw won his first assignment, but refused to pitch for East Homer again unless the manager gave him $5 a game and paid for a horse-drawn hack to take him to the ballpark and back home.

After considerable argument, the manager agreed.

When McGraw continued to win at East Homer, a Truxton man named A. F. "Bert" Kenney offered him a job with Olean in the New York-Penn League. Kenney, the manager of the team, said the pay would be $60 a month plus board.

Even though his father objected, McGraw went to Olean. After all, Olean represented the answer to his prayers and dreams. He would now be a "professional" player.

From the very beginning of his career, John McGraw displayed a complex personality marked by four strong characteristics — courage, determination, self-confidence and ego.

When McGraw reported to Olean, for example, he had visions of pitching himself into the Majors before the end of the season. Unfortunately, Manager Kenney put the 17-year-old on third base. His debut was a disaster.

After six games, he was benched because he couldn't hit the first baseman after fielding a ground ball.

Undaunted, McGraw jumped to Wellsville in the Western New York League. There, he started as a pitcher but was shifted to the infield. To avoid another benching, McGraw worked hard, improved his fielding and batted .365 in 24 games.

After the 1890 season, McGraw joined a group of Minor League all-stars on a barnstorming trip. During the swing, he starred in an exhibition game against the National League Cleveland Spiders. That performance led to a contract to play for Cedar Rapids in the Three-I League (Illinois, Indiana and Iowa).

Early the next season, Cedar Rapids played an exhibition game against Chicago, now dubbed the "Colts." In his first time at bat, McGraw singled to right field. When he reached first base, McGraw needled Cap Anson, the first baseman, "Hey, old timer, is that what you call big league pitching? We're gon'a murder him."

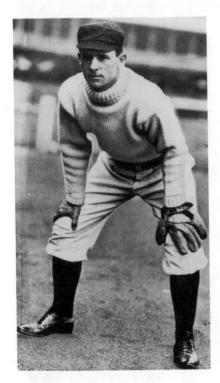

John McGraw, a runt with big ears and a big mouth, got off to a bad start as a professional ballplayer.

Anson, still in his prime and one of the biggest stars of the game at the time, stared in disbelief at the audacious 120-pound teenager.

Realizing that he had gotten under Anson's skin, McGraw kept badgering the great first baseman.

At the same time, he led the team in batting and handled 11 fielding plays flawlessly at shortstop.

After the game, Anson took McGraw aside, complimented him on his play and asked whether he would like to join the Chicago club someday. Overwhelmed by attracting such attention from Anson, McGraw admitted later that the encounter "went to my head immediately."

"All thoughts of the Three-I League were forgotten," he said in his autobiography. "I would be a big leaguer or nothing."

That summer, his manager, Bill Gleason, said he'd gotten a letter from Billie Barnie, the manager of the Baltimore Orioles.

"Barnie wants to know how good you are," Gleason said.

Cocky as always, McGraw responded, "Well, you can tell him I'm just about as good as they come."

Although baseball didn't know it yet, this brash, self-sufficient and determined bantamweight of a ballplayer would, like Harry Wright, blaze a new trail for baseball as it moved into another era.

23 A New Weapon

WHEN JOHN MCGRAW reported to Baltimore in the middle of the 1891 season, Manager Billie Barnie couldn't believe his eyes. "Why, you're just a kid!" Barnie exploded.

"Just put me out there and I'll show you I can play," McGraw shot back, jutting his chin at Barnie.

Barnie gave McGraw the chance he asked for and through the rest of the season he played in 33 games, mostly at shortstop, and batted .383.

Early the following year, however, McGraw was benched as the American Association merged with the National League and Baltimore was absorbed in the National's 12-team circuit.

The team dropped to last place and Ned Hanlon was brought in to manage. His arrival marked a turning point in McGraw's life.

Hanlon, experimenting with what he had inherited, used McGraw as a utility infielder. In his first game off the bench, against Chicago,

McGraw was so impressive Anson tried to trade an outfielder for him right then and there, but Hanlon refused.

During the season, Hanlon wanted more experience in the infield and traded for Cub Stricker. This bumped McGraw out of the lineup and Hanlon decided to send the scrappy youngster to a Minor League club in Mobile, Alabama.

McGraw balked. He told Hanlon he'd rather sit on the bench with the Orioles than be farmed out. Hanlon relented. But instead of sitting on the bench, McGraw, playing several positions as Hanlon's first substitute, appeared in 79 games and batted .344.

Over the winter months, Hanlon began to build for the future. He started with three players: catcher Wilbert Robinson, pitcher John "Sadie" McMahon and the Orioles' new third baseman, John McGraw.

Later, Hanlon added outfielders Joe Kelley, Wee Willie Keeler, shortstop Hughie Jennings and second baseman Kid Gleason.

The Orioles, last in 1892 in the 12-team league, finished eighth in '93.

By this time, McGraw, ever fearful of being dropped to the Minors, had developed into the team's driving spirit. But he coupled his rapidly improving play with the worst kind of behavior imaginable.

He relentlessly cursed umpires, players and fans alike. He also used all sorts of "dirty" tactics—kicking the ball out of the hands of opposing players, spiking anyone in his way, grabbing runners by the belt when the umpires weren't looking—anything and everything that would help the Orioles win and keep him in the Majors.

Despite his pugnacious, rowdy behavior, which prompted a disgusted sportswriter to refer to him as "Mugs," McGraw was a serious student of baseball and constantly experimented with new tactics and new plays. And wherever he played, he knew more about the rules than anyone else.

By the time the new pitching distance went into effect in 1894, Ned Hanlon had completed his rebuilding of the Orioles, a team that changed baseball with what became known as the "scientific" or "inside" game.

Today, it is a routine part of diamond play, drilled into players from Little League on up to the Majors.

Some who saw the Orioles of that day insist the team had only one great star—Wee Willie Keller. Like McGraw, Keeler batted from the left side of the plate, even though he threw with his right hand. But he was smaller than McGraw, standing only 5 feet 4.

Keeler, who used a 31½-inch bat, the shortest ever seen in the Majors, was an outstanding batter and baserunner. Once, when asked what advice he had to give younger players, Keeler responded, "Keep your eye clear and hit 'em where they ain't."

What the Orioles may have lacked in skill, they more than made up for with teamwork. On defense, they introduced the tactic of shading right or left to offset the strength of hitters. They also were the first to utilize a set of signals for all offensive and defensive maneuvers.

With the pitcher now moved back an additional 10½ feet, they employed the bunt extensively — in particular the squeeze bunt. They also used the hit-and-run whenever possible.

Most of all, the team relied on speed to move the defense and score runs. McGraw, for example, stole 78 bases in 1894, second highest in the League.

As a team, the Orioles stole 324 bases, only three fewer than Chicago, the League leader.

The first club to get a taste of the style of play inaugurated by the Orioles was the New York Giants, managed by John Ward.

At first, Ward thought some of the things happening on the diamond came about accidentally. But after the Orioles completed 13 hit-and-run plays as they swept a four-game series — with McGraw driving in the winning run in the ninth inning of the last game — Ward conceded that the Orioles had brought something new to baseball.

Others dismissed the Oriole tactics as "kid stuff" when word got around the League during the spring. By season's end, however, there was a change of opinion as the Orioles won 24 of their last 25 games on a trip through the West and finished first, three games ahead of the Giants.

The Baltimore Orioles, managed by John McGraw (hatless, center), **became the greatest exponent of the "inside" or "scientific" game.**

The Orioles' "scientific" game continued to pay dividends as they won the Championship the following two years.

The one play that the Orioles mastered and brought into general use was the hit-and-run. And while the team used this play extensively, it was McGraw batting behind his close friend, Hughie Jennings, and Keeler batting behind McGraw, who popularized it.

No other offensive weapon matched the hit-and-run until Babe Ruth exploded on the scene with 29 homers in 1919.

24 Same Horse, Another Race

J OHN McGRAW WASN'T in the Majors very long before he began dreaming of managing his own ballclub.

He got his chance when Ned Hanlon and Harry Von der Horst, owner of the Orioles, formed a syndicate after the 1898 season that gave them ownership of both the Orioles and Brooklyn.

Hanlon and Von der Horst had what they thought was a profitable idea: Since the Orioles weren't making money in Baltimore, they would keep the franchise but move the best players to Brooklyn.

McGraw and the Orioles' catcher, Wilbert Robinson, however, were partners in a local business, the Diamond Cafe, and refused to leave Baltimore. As a result, McGraw was named manager of the Baltimore club, while Robinson remained to catch and serve as his assistant.

Although Hanlon and his aggregation of former Orioles and other stars easily won the pennant, McGraw's team of castoffs finished fourth.

McGraw, playing third base and batting fourth, had an exceptional year. He racked up a .391 batting average, third highest in the League; drew a League-leading 124 walks; and ranked second with 73 stolen bases and 140 runs scored.

He also developed outfielder Jimmy Sheckard and pitcher Joe McGinnity, players Hanlon had decided he didn't want.

McGinnity won 28 games, which tied him with the League leader in games won, while Sheckard was tops with 77 stolen bases.

The 26-year-old McGraw's sparkling play and astonishing success as a first-year manager drew a great deal of attention, and he received a number of offers. But, at first, Hanlon and Von der Horst refused to let him go.

One of the reasons, of course, was that the Baltimore branch of the syndicate made a profit in 1899, while Brooklyn ended up in the red.

Stanley and Fred Robison, owners of the Cleveland franchise, also formed a syndicate and bought the St. Louis club. But, this too, failed.

For a long time, those who operated baseball couldn't decide why attendance kept dropping. Some thought it was the new bicycle craze that was sweeping the nation. Others thought it was something else new— motion pictures, or the "flickers."

The outbreak of the Spanish-American War, coupled with a recession, definitely cut into attendance at ballgames. But the basic problem was that the League was topheavy and dominated by two teams, as the following indicates: In 1892, Boston won the Championship; in 1893, it was Boston again; in 1894, 95 and 96, it was Baltimore; and in 1897 and 98, it was Boston again with Baltimore finishing second both times.

In an attempt to stimulate more interest in the game, League officials first introduced the post-season games for the Dauvray Cup. In a best-of-seven contest, the first place team would take on the runner-up.

When Boston retired the Dauvray cup after three series victories, a Pittsburgh sportsman named William Temple put up another cup. Although Baltimore won the flag in 1894, John Ward's Giants whipped the Orioles four straight to capture the first Temple Cup.

Baltimore, however, won the next three.

Still, attendance dropped off, convincing many that the circuit had to be reduced from 12 to eight teams.

As soon as it became evident that this might happen, an effort was made to revive the American Association.

McGraw, who was promised a role in the Baltimore franchise, supported the move along with Wilbert Robinson and Adrian "Cap" Anson, who had been let go by Chicago.

The attempt failed, however, when several would-be owners backed out of the deal.

As the 1900 season approached, the National bought out four clubs—Baltimore, Cleveland, Louisville and Washington—and reverted to an eight-team loop.

All of the Baltimore players were ordered to report to Hanlon and if not cut from the squad would play for Brooklyn.

Again, McGraw and Robinson refused.

After getting permission from Brooklyn to talk with the pair, Fred Robison offered them jobs in St. Louis.

In the belief that the American Association would be back in business the following year and that the Baltimore job would be his, McGraw said he would accept on three conditions: that the contract be for one year; that the reserve clause be stricken; and that they could agree on a salary. Robinson took the same position.

After some dickering, Robison agreed. He signed McGraw for $9,500, which was believed to be the highest salary offered any player at the time.

The American Association, with its promised Baltimore franchise, never came into existence. But another league did. And John McGraw found himself riding his favorite horse in another race.

25 Winners All

WHEN BYRON BANCROFT JOHNSON graduated from Marietta College in Ohio, his parents expected him to become a minister and educator like other male members of the family, including his father.

But Johnson, a deep-chested, rugged man, had other ideas. While at Marietta, he caught for the college team and had fallen in love with baseball. And since he didn't have the ability or desire to make it as a professional player, he did the next best thing; he took a job with the *Cincinnati Commercial Gazette* and wrote about baseball.

A brilliant and forceful individual, Johnson was a constant critic of baseball's hierarchy, in particular the owner of the Cincinnati Reds, John T. Brush, author of the Classification Plan that led to the Brotherhood Revolt.

Inevitably, while covering the Reds in 1892, Johnson met Charles Comiskey, the Cincinnati club's new manager. Comiskey was 33 at the time and Johnson was 28. Comiskey had won four championships in a row managing the St. Louis Browns and had taken the Chicago entry in the Players League to a fourth place finish. He was not fond of the National League; neither was Johnson.

The two became fast friends, though Johnson continued to take pot-shots at Brush in his news articles.

Johnson and Comiskey would often meet in saloons, both in Cincinnati and on the road, and discuss baseball. A favorite topic was the tenuous state of the game. Eventually, the two decided that what baseball needed was a new Major League.

The idea began to take root while Comiskey was on a scouting trip in the South and Midwest and ran into several people who wanted to revive the defunct Western Association. Comiskey persuaded the group

Pittsburgh's Connie Mack was one of many stars Ban Johnson lured to the new American League with the promise of higher pay and better working conditions.

to establish the circuit among the small cities around Chicago and to consider Ban Johnson to head up the organization.

During the winter of 1894, Johnson and Comiskey attended the first organizational meeting of the Western League backers — Johnson as a reporter and Comiskey as an informal advisor. It was agreed that the new loop would include Sioux City (Iowa), Toledo, Indianapolis, Detroit, Kansas City, Milwaukee, Minneapolis and Grand Rapids.

When the highly respected Comiskey took the floor and recommended Johnson as the new President of the League, the vote was unanimous. Johnson took over as soon as he arranged for a one-year leave of absence from his paper.

By the time the new league's season ended, Johnson had proved he knew how to manage a baseball league. Every franchise made money, which prompted Johnson to cut his ties with the *Gazette*.

Johnson's success with the Western League also induced Comiskey to leave Cincinnati and take over the Sioux City franchise, which he quickly moved to St. Paul. At the same time, Johnson persuaded Connie Mack, who had managed Pittsburgh in 1896, to buy into the Milwaukee franchise.

For the next few years the Western League operators concentrated on building up their League, but three events spurred Johnson forward with plans to form a new Major League.

The first of these developments was the decision by the National League to cut four teams from their 12-club circuit.

The second was the attempt to revive the American Association.

And the third was the simple fact that a five-year agreement between the Western League and the National League had expired.

When these three things occurred, Johnson knew the time was ripe to make his move.

In October 1899 he began by renaming his organization the American League. Then, with the permission of the National League, he moved one franchise into Cleveland and Comiskey into Chicago with another.

A few weeks later, Nick Young, Secretary of the National League, wired Johnson and asked him to forward his dues for the continued protection of his League under the National Agreement. Johnson, in response, made it clear that the American was no longer a Minor League and that it was "unreasonable to assume we can continue along the old lines prescribed by the National Agreement."

Johnson also stated that the American planned to "extend our circuit to the far East" in 1901. He said, however, that he hoped to do so without sparking another baseball war.

It was his view that things could be worked out peacefully at the National League's winter meetings in New York.

Anticipating a call to the meeting, Johnson and a committee of American Leaguers situated themselves nearby and waited.

The call never came. Johnson's response was:

"If they want war, they'll have it."

And war it was, the fifth in 12 years.

Oddly enough, it was a war in which everyone eventually became a winner.

26 David and Goliath

WHEN BAN JOHNSON decided to put the American League on an equal footing with the National, the odds against him seemed overwhelming.

Consider the following:

- His opponent was a battle-scarred, crafty veteran that had overcome all sorts of adversity and survived four crippling wars over a 24-year period.
- He needed money.

Al Reach, one of baseball's earliest pros, was President of the Philadelphia Phillies while his partner in a sporting-goods business, Ben Shibe, owned the Philadelphia Athletics.

- He needed new ballparks.
- He needed capable field managers.
- He needed players with Major League ability.
- He had less than a year to reach his goals.

An ordinary man would have quailed at the thought of overcoming so many obstacles. But Ban Johnson was no ordinary man. Moving with remarkable speed, he persuaded Charlie Somers, a wealthy coal and shipping magnate and backer of the Cleveland club, to help fund some of the new teams.

With Somers' financial support, Johnson then lined up others to join his venture. In Philadelphia, for example, he was able to convince Ben Shibe to take over the new American League franchise in that city.

Shibe was a partner in the sporting goods business founded by Al Reach, the owner of the Phillies. To clinch the deal, Johnson gave the Reach company an exclusive contract to supply the American League with baseballs.

As a result, one partner owned the National League Phillies, while the other was the backer of the American League Athletics.

In addition to Philadelphia, Johnson added Washington, Baltimore and Boston to his circuit.

As he rounded up backers, Johnson paired them with "name" managers, most of whom also invested in the clubs they joined.

John McGraw, a free agent after the 1900 season with St. Louis, moved East again to take over a new American League franchise in Baltimore.

Connie Mack went to the Athletics, Hugh Duffy to Milwaukee and Jim Manning took over Washington.

The legendary Cy Young joined the wave of National League stars who jumped to Ban Johnson's new circuit.

As the two rival leagues approached the 1901 season, the lineup of the franchises looked like this:

American League	National League
Chicago	Chicago
Boston	Boston
Philadelphia	Philadelphia
Detroit	New York
Baltimore	Pittsburgh
Washington	Brooklyn
Cleveland	St. Louis
Milwaukee	Cincinnati

While Johnson's selection of managers was of enormous help in gaining the support of the money men who were interested in baseball, it was also instrumental in luring many of the National's stars to the new loop.

McGraw, for example, easily signed some of his old Orioles, including Joe McGinnity, who had pitched Brooklyn to the pennant in 1900 with a League-leading 28 victories.

To make the American League attractive to National League players, Johnson did three things:

**A court order obtained by the Phillies
kept Napoleon Lajoie out of Philadelphia.**

1. He offered more money.
2. He refused to adopt the National's policy of putting a $2,000
   ceiling on salaries.
3. He recognized the Players Protective Association, a new union
   formed by the players—something the National would not do.

Johnson's tactics were so successful that he was able to convince
scores of the National's best players to join his league.

Among those who made the switch was the sensational Cy Young,
who left St. Louis to sign with Boston, where he proceeded to win 33
games while losing 10, the top pitching performance in the League.

The most celebrated jumper at the time, however, was Napoleon Lajoie,
the Phillies' hard-hitting, slick-fielding second baseman. Offered a little
more money to join Connie Mack's Athletics, Lajoie quickly signed a
contract.

The Phillies retaliated by fighting the case right up to the Pennsylvania Supreme Court. The court found in the Phillies' favor, saying
that the loss of Lajoie would cause the team irreparable harm. The
court consequently issued an order that prevented Lajoie from playing
with the Athletics.

Ban Johnson got around the ruling by simply arranging to have Lajoie
transferred to Cleveland. While on the Cleveland roster, Lajoie stayed
out of Pennsylvania, missing the games his club played in Philadelphia
against the As.

While the Nationals sued in other state courts, the rulings went against them.

Johnson's battle to establish the American League was not limited to legal and other skirmishes with his National League opponents.

First and foremost, he was determined to make American League games the most attractive in baseball. Like William Hulbert, Harry Wright and Al Spalding before him, Johnson was an advocate of "clean" baseball and baseball that was free of foul language and rowdy behavior. To achieve his goals, he gave his umpires unprecedented authority on the field and backed them to the hilt.

By the end of the 1901 season, it became clear that David had taken the measure of Goliath and a new Major League had been born.

27 The Villain and the Hero

I N A BIZARRE EFFORT to increase profits and thwart Ban Johnson and the American League, four of the National League's eight owners got together in August of 1901 and hatched a plot that surely would have killed professional baseball had it succeeded.

The conspirators included Andrew Freedman, owner of the New York Giants, Frank Robison of St. Louis, Arthur Soden of Boston and John T. Brush of Cincinnati.

Freedman, the architect of the scheme, was a young, brilliant real estate operator and insurance broker who had strong connections to New York's corrupt Tammany Hall, bastion of the ruling Democratic Party.

He was also, without doubt, the most hated man in baseball; hated by his peers, hated by the fans, hated by sportswriters and hated by his players. And for good reason. He abused his players, ignored the interests of the fans and fought continuously with sportswriters, League officials and other owners.

On one occasion, he physically attacked Brush, an older and smaller man, in a New York restaurant. On another, he rushed from his private box onto the field and ordered an umpire to eject Baltimore's Jim "Ducky" Holmes from a game after he overheard the player refer to him as a "sheeny." The umpire refused because he hadn't heard this ethnic slur. The furious Freedman then called on the police to eject Holmes. The umpire, however, waved Freedman off the field and yelled, "Play ball!"

When Freedman wouldn't allow the Giants to take the field, the ump promptly forfeited the game to Baltimore, a move that brought a wave of cheers from the 3,000 fans attending the game.

Hundreds of fans then swarmed out of the stands to surround Freedman and demand that he refund their money. At first he refused, but when the crowd became more aggressive, he relented.

Freedman, who was 34 at the time, got into baseball by buying out the stock Al Spalding owned in the New York Giants. (Spalding and others, including his brother, J. Walter Spalding, John Brush and Arthur Soden, it will be recalled, obtained shares of stock in the Giants when they pooled $80,000 to keep the New York club from going under during the war with the Players League.)

At Freedman's insistence, J. Walter Spalding held onto a few of his shares and became a director of the New York club. J. Walter became so disgusted with Freedman's language, conduct and methods of doing business, however, that he soon resigned.

Despite his abrasive personality, Freedman, a bachelor and a millionaire, was a master at putting together complicated deals.

The plan he unveiled at his summer home in Red Bank, New Jersey, was called "syndicatism" and was well known in business circles. His proposal, to which his co-conspirators agreed despite their personal feelings about Freedman, boiled down to this:

- The National Agreement would be scrapped.
- In its place the owners would create a new organization called the National League Trust.
- Five men, designated as a Board of Regents, would be in control of the organization.
- The Board would select the President, Treasurer and Secretary and appoint the field managers, all of whom would receive the same salary.
- The Board would assign the players to each team and fix their salaries.
- The Board would also place the teams in cities of its choosing.
- The syndicate would issue preferred and common stock. The preferred stock, shared by all, would pay a dividend of 7 percent.

To assure themselves control, the Freedman group would receive the majority of the common, or voting, stock.

The New York club (Freedman) was to receive 30 percent of the common stock, while Cincinnati (Brush), Boston (Soden) and St. Louis (Robison) would each receive 12 percent. The other four clubs were to receive from 6 to 10 percent.

With 66 percent of the voting stock, the Freedman group would in effect have complete control of the entire organization, including the eight teams. The objective, of course, was to manage the syndicate in a way that would maximize profits.

Basically, this was an expansion of the idea the Robison brothers, Ned Hanlon and Harry Von der Horst had when they controlled teams in both Cleveland and St. Louis and in Baltimore and Brooklyn. But, instead of one owner holding two franchises, the magnates would join together to own ALL the clubs in the syndicate.

This meant, of course, that the teams would lose their identity; that players and clubs could be moved about at the whim of the Board of Regents; and that prices and salaries could be controlled.

Worst of all, "competition" could be contrived and manipulated by stocking two cities with the best players one year and moving them to two different cities the next, and so on.

Freedman and his group hoped to spring the syndicate plan on the other unsuspecting owners at the winter meetings and ram it through for approval. Fortunately for baseball, the story broke in the newspapers just prior to the meeting, sparking a wave of disapproval. It also prompted the panicky and desperate anti-Freedman group to call on the one man they felt had the prestige, power and brains to kill syndicate baseball:

Albert Goodwill Spalding.

When Spalding accepted the challenge, the stage was set for a classic duel between the Villain and the Hero.

28 The Gauntlet Is Thrown

ALTHOUGH AL SPALDING had put himself on baseball's sidelines 10 years before Andrew Freedman's syndicate plan exploded in the nation's sports pages, he always managed to keep abreast of what was going on.

During that 10-year span, A. G. Spalding and Brothers had grown enormously. It had 10 large factories operating in various parts of the country and, in addition to its catalog business, had 14 outlets for the huge volume of sporting goods the factories produced.

As if that weren't enough to keep him busy, Spalding had also organized the American Bicycle Company during that period, to capitalize on a bicycle craze that was sweeping the country.

Even though these extensive business interests occupied most of his attention, Spalding was in frequent contact with various owners of League clubs. When war broke out with the American League, he was urged, unofficially, to intercede with Ban Johnson. He did meet with Johnson on one occasion and learned that Johnson would be amenable to a peaceful settlement with the National.

While Spalding favored the development of the two leagues, however, Freedman and other hard-liners did not. Seing that his efforts in that direction would be wasted, he dropped further contact with Johnson.

When the reported attempt to turn baseball into a trust and the subsequent call for help from the anti-Freedman group developed, however, the 51-year-old Spalding canceled his appointments and rushed to New York to attend the League's winter conference, which was to be held December 11 at the Fifth Avenue Hotel.

On entering the League meeting room, he learned that he had been nominated for President by Barney Dreyfuss of Pittsburgh. Frank Robison, however, had objected, saying that the 10-year-old National Agreement was to expire that very night and, before a President could be elected, the League would have to be reorganized. Presumably, if all had agreed with Robison, the plan for the National Baseball Trust would have been introduced.

While Freedman, Brush and Soden voted with Robison, the other four owners—Dreyfuss, Charlie Ebbets of Brooklyn, Al Reach of Philadelphia and Jim Hart of Chicago—were opposed.

With the meeting deadlocked, an emotional Spalding addressed the gathering, "Gentlemen, I was present at the birth of this organization. I saw it when its eyes were first opened to the light of day, 26 years ago next February, in this city.

"If it is to be buried today—if this is its last day—I ask, gentlemen, the privilege of closing its eyes in death. I claim that not only as a privilege but a right.

"I also want to be here to take away the body, that an autopsy may be held to determine the cause of death. I also claim that I have a right to say something about where it shall be buried and I may have something to offer as to the design of the monument erected over it."

Spalding went on to point out that the National League had "two fathers."

"One," he said, was "William A. Hulbert—God bless his memory—and the other, myself."

He noted that 26 years earlier he and Hulbert wrote the League's constitution and that gave him the right to speak out in the meeting.

". . . some of the best friends I have in the world are here," he told the group. "But when it comes to the question of personal friendship for one of you, or two of you, or all of you combined, I think more of the National League than I do of any one of you or all of you."

He said the whole country was watching, because "people have the idea that you are a band of conspirators, talking nothing but gate receipts."

He then scolded the owners for getting into a fight with the American League, losing its players and the support of the public and the newspapers.

In conclusion, he said that he was not seeking the Presidency of the League and had not given anyone authority to propose his name for that office.

After the meeting, Freedman told newsmen that Spalding had been "defeated" for the Presidency.

"Four years ago, when asked to come back, he said he was out of baseball for good," Freedman said. "At that time bicycling was a great sport and baseball second . . . It is all well for Spalding when new contracts are to be given out for baseballs. But when he meets with opposition, he rushes to the newspapers.

"I say he has done nothing for baseball that baseball hasn't done for him."

The next morning, despite Spalding's stated position, a local newspaper reported the meeting was deadlocked because of his efforts to get himself elected President.

Fuming with indignation, Spalding promptly called a press conference to set the record straight. Standing before the more than 50 newsmen, Spalding, who now weighed well over 200 pounds, was an impressive figure as he pounded his fists and waved his arms to make his points. Mincing no words, he repeated that he had not sought election as League President, but that if he were elected, he would only accept on one condition:

Freedman would have to be "eleminated from the councils" of the League.

And then, shaking a fist and rocking up on his toes while perspiration dripped down his face and off his chin, he added, "The issue is now between Andrew Freedman and A. G. Spalding and when I get back actively into baseball, Andrew Freedman gets out. He gets out right away, or I'll get out!"

The writers, as one newspaper reported, "were thrilled as if by electric shock and after recovering their equilibrium, a great shout went up and then there was a mad scramble among the scribes to shake Spalding by the hand and congratulate him."

The gauntlet had been thrown, but the battle had yet to be won.

29 The Saviour

THE STALEMATE over the election of a new President of the National League in December of 1901 continued for three days. And when the clock in the lobby of the Fifth Avenue Hotel ticked by 1:00 in the morning on December 14, there was every reason to believe the deadlock would continue through at least one more day, or even longer.

For by the 13th, Spalding's supporters had nominated him no less than 25 times. And 25 times, when the nomination was put to a vote, the ballots added up just as they had over the three previous days: four votes for Spalding and four votes for the incumbent, Nicholas Young.

Sometime between one and two o'clock that morning, however, Freedman and his clique, wearied by the hours and days of wrangling over this single issue, left the meeting room before adjournment was called and without permission of Nick Young who, as President, chaired the session.

After a few moments, the helpless and exhausted Young also left.

John Rogers, representing the Phillies, then took the chair and called for still another vote.

This time, it was 4 to 0 in favor of Spalding. The meeting was then quickly adjourned.

After the spurious election, matters moved swiftly. Spalding was awakened and filled in on what had happened. Delighted at this humorous and unexpected turn of events, Spalding promptly dressed and went to rooms occupied by Nick Young and his son, Robert. After awakening the pair, Spalding boldly announced he was the new President of the National League and demanded the League records.

Groggy with sleep, Nick Young argued briefly with Spalding, then told Robert to take care of the records, which were in a trunk in his room, and went back to bed. Spalding left and, an hour later, was back, accompanied by a porter.

As he again wrangled with Robert, he signaled the porter to seize the trunkful of records and take them to his hotel. Concerned for his weary and aging father's health and not too sure of his own ground, Robert let Spalding go.

When the meeting was re-convened later that day so the League could get on with its regular business, Spalding took the chair. He and his four backers were the only occupants of the meeting room at the time.

Watching the proceedings from the doorway, however, was Fred Knowles, Freedman's co-delegate and Secretary of the Giants.

Spalding blithely called the roll. To establish a quorum, he had the stenographer note that Knowles was "present."

As soon as the meeting was over, Spalding announced his election to the press. He also told reporters that he had invited Freedman to meet with him the following afternoon to debate "the baseball situation." According to his autobiography, Spalding called that meeting to order at the appointed hour and asked Freedman to step forward.

There was no response.

"Very seriously, I explained my great surprise and disappointment that the President of the New York club was not present to represent the cause of the proposed Base Ball Trust," Spalding wrote. ". . . However, I felt that, being there, I ought to say something in behalf of a game its enemies were seeking to kill."

Spalding again castigated Freedman and his group. The absent Freedman was quick to retaliate. As Spalding left the meeting room, a "dapper little fellow" handed him a court summons and said, "Mr. Spalding, you've been enjoined."

Spalding quickly handed the paper to his lawyer and left the state, soon journeying to his new home in California.

The Spalding-Freedman battle paralyzed the League for the next several months. During that period, Spalding tried again to settle the war with the American League.

While Ban Johnson was willing, he pointed out that Spalding represented only four clubs and a settlement would be meaningless.

As spring approached, both sides realized that something had to be done. After a meeting to set up the schedule for the 1902 season, the League delegates came up with a compromise that Jim Hart, Spalding's successor as President of the Chicago White Stockings, took to Spalding in California.

Here is the plan Hart unveiled. If Spalding would resign, Freedman would sell his interest in the Giants to John Brush and get out of baseball; Brush would sell his interest in Cincinnati to a local group headed by a newcomer, August "Garry" Herrmann, and the syndicate plan would be dropped.

Without the slightest hesitation, Spalding took pen in hand and resigned from the office he never held.

Nevertheless, to maintain the fiction that he was still President, Spalding asked Hart to hold onto the letter of resignation until he was sure Freedman had parted company with baseball.

During his lifetime, Al Spalding made many important contributions to baseball. He played a key role in the establishment of the National League (and Hall of Fame); standardized the ball and other equipment; and helped lead baseball out of the Brotherhood and two other wars.

He was also baseball's greatest missionary, climaxing his tireless efforts to promote the game by writing and producing the first complete

Al Spalding saved baseball from disaster— not once, but twice.

history of baseball, *America's National Game*. Published in 1911, the 600-page book—partly autobiography and personal opinion—contains a great deal of documentation of the early game and has become a valuable information source for historians and others.

Spalding, who died September 9, 1915, at age 65, dedicated his book to the National League; to Henry Chadwick as the "Father" of baseball; and to William Hulbert as the "Saviour" of baseball.

But if anyone deserves the title of "Saviour," it is Al Spalding, as the elimination of Freedmanism alone clearly indicates.

30 The Feud

WHEN JOHN McGRAW and Ban Johnson joined forces, it was clearly a marriage of convenience.

McGraw wanted to be a manager and at least part-owner of a major League club, not an aging third baseman for the weak St. Louis Cardinals.

Johnson, on the other hand, wanted an American League that would be more powerful than the National at the gate and on the playing field. McGraw, a major prize, represented a big boost in that direction.

Thus, when the two first met in Chicago toward the end of 1900, the situation boiled down to this: Johnson needed McGraw and McGraw needed Johnson.

But after one year—a year in which Baltimore finished fifth, 13 games behind Clark Griffith's Chicago champions—it was clear the honeymoon was over.

McGraw, fighting to move his club up in the standings, ran head-on into Johnson's adamant policy against rowdyism on the diamond. Time and again, McGraw was thrown out of ballgames and fined and suspended for abusing umpires. And time and again, Johnson backed the umps and ignored McGraw's arguments that he was right and the umpires were wrong.

As is usually the case when two strong-willed men clash, something had to give.

Early in 1902, a series of events paved the way to the end of the Johnson-McGraw relationship. It began when the Orioles slipped into last place. While the club lost money in 1901, it became obvious that it would lose even more money in its second year in the American League.

It also became obvious that Ban Johnson felt Baltimore couldn't support a Major League team and was ready to drop the Orioles and move the franchise to New York.

Because of his constant battles with Johnson, McGraw knew he wasn't included in Johnson's plans, though he ached to manage in the nation's largest city.

Some time in June, McGraw called the Baltimore stockholders together to discuss his deteriorating situation. According to his book *My Thirty Years in Baseball,* McGraw addressed the group as follows.

"Gentlemen, I have advanced the club nearly $7,000 to keep it going. The company is in debt to me that much personally. Now, I think I should be paid that money back or given my unconditional release."

As McGraw anticipated, he was given his release.

Shortly after McGraw's ultimatum to the Baltimore stockholders, Fred Knowles, Secretary of the New York Giants, went to Baltimore for meeting with McGraw while he was again under suspension.

Knowles said that Andrew Freedman, who was still in control of the Giants at the time, would like him to manage the New York club.

McGraw saw this as a golden opportunity, even though the Giants were in last place. But, as usual, McGraw was crafty.

Knowing that Freedman often interfered with his managers and fired them at the slightest provocation, he said he would accept the offer only if certain conditions were written into the contract. These conditions would give him:

- Absolute control on the field.
- Absolute authority to trade, buy or release players.
- A four-year contract of $11,000.

With the pitching of Christy Mathewson (left) and Joe McGinnity (right), John McGraw's Giants surged from last to first in the National League.

Freedman knew he would soon be giving up the Giants to John Brush as a result of the compromise with the supporters of Al Spalding, and agreed to the terms without a quibble.

When the story broke in the newpapers on July 10, it caused quite a sensation. Giant fans, of course, were delighted, as the 29-year-old McGraw was regarded as the best playing manager in baseball.

But matters didn't end there. Since the war with the American League was still going on, McGraw took five of his best Baltimore players to New York with him, including Joe McGinnity and Roger Bresnahan, one of the best all-round players in the game.

When Johnson learned of McGraw's defection, he promptly labeled the fiery little thirdsacker a "traitor" and a "Benedict Arnold."

Never one to ignore a challenge, McGraw blasted back in kind.

The Pittsburgh Pirates made a shambles of the pennant race in 1902, finishing 27½ games in front of second-place Brooklyn and 55 games ahead of McGraw's last-place Giants.

McGraw's first full year with the Giants, however, was a different story. Like his former mentor, Ned Hanlon, McGraw knew how to build a team, and over the winter he concentrated on revamping the Giants.

The team to beat, obviously, was the powerful Pittsburgh club. But the Pirates, with an offense built around a sensational shortstop named Honus Wagner (.335) and manager Fred Clarke (.351), still managed to stay on top. The Giants, however, startled the League by moving from last the year before to second place, just six games behind Pittsburgh.

They owed their success to a combination of excellent fielding—the best in the league—and fine pitching. The ever-loyal Joe McGinnity, for example, won 32 and lost 18, while another right-hander, Christy

Mathewson, won 29 while losing 12. As for McGraw, he benched himself in favor of Billy Lauder and appeared in but 12 games.

While 1902 virtually marked the end of McGraw's playing days, it launched one of the greatest managerial careers in baseball history. And since McGraw and Johnson never spoke to each other again, it also signaled the start of a feud that lasted almost 30 years.

31 Recognition Plus

I N ITS FIRST two years of operation, the American league lured more than 100 National League players to its ranks to fill a total roster of about 125.

With the help of so many National League players, 25¢ admissions (as contrasted to 50¢ in the National) and fairly close pennant races, the American League not only made money, but began to outdraw the National.

Still, the National refused to recognize the American as a Major League.

But late in 1902, as John McGraw had anticipated, Johnson was able to quietly shift the Baltimore franchise to New York.

For two years, Andrew Freedman's friends in City Hall made it clear that if and when Johnson decided to build a ballpark in New York, he would soon learn that the land would be condemned for construction of a new street or streetcar line.

When Freedman finally got out of baseball and Johnson agreed to accept Frank Farrell and Bill Devery as part owners of the New York franchise, that obstacle was cleared since Farrell was a crony of Tammany Boss Dick Croker and Devery was the former Chief of Police.

Pushing ahead, Johnson helped the new owners acquire a piece of property of 168th Street and Broadway. Plans were then made to construct a ballfield and a wooden stand that would seat 10,000 people. The new team (ultimately the New York Yankees) was to be named Highlanders, and the popular Clark Griffith was signed up as its first manager.

All of this news broke toward the end of the summer and was followed by announcements that several more National League players were leaving their teams to join the American.

Wee Willie Keeler, for example, left Brooklyn to play for the Highlanders for an unprecedented offer of $10,000. Two of the Pirates' best pitchers—Jack Chesbro and Jesse Tannehill—also jumped to the Highlanders. Still more startling was the New York Giants' loss of catcher Frank Bowerman and pitcher Christy Mathewson to the St. Louis Browns.

By the time of the annual fall convention, the National League, which had been under the direction of John Brush, Arthur Soden and Jim Hart ever since the Al Spalding-Nick Young debacle, had had enough.

The delegates elected 33-year-old Harry C. Pulliam, a former newsman who was Secretary of the Pittsburgh club, as President.

Although John Brush wanted to continue the fight with his old enemy, the rest of the owners made it clear that Pulliam's first order of business was to find a way to end the war with Johnson and the American League.

The energetic Pulliam lost no time in going into action, appointing a committee to meet with the Johnson group in January 1903. At that meeting, the Nationals proposed absorbing the best American League clubs and reverting to another 12-team circuit.

Johnson and his friends flatly refused this approach and walked out of the meeting.

Later, after a few preliminary contacts with Johnson, Pulliam appointed himself to a committee of two with August Herrmann and shortly thereafter met in Cincinnati with Johnson and Charles Comiskey to work out peace terms.

In meetings that lasted two full days, the four men fashioned an agreement that covered all of baseball, including the National Association of Baseball Leagues (the Minors).

Based primarily on the so-called "baseball law" written originally by Abraham Mills, the agreement contained the following major provisions:

- The three parties to the agreement were separate entities and would operate independently.
- The same playing rules would apply to all.
- Territorial rights and all player contracts would be honored.
- All Major League games would be scheduled with a minimum of conflict.
- With the exception of salaries, Major League player contracts would be identical.
- The National and the American leagues were to have equal status.

In a significant departure from the original National Agreement, however, it was decided to appoint a National Commission to enforce the "law," a sort of Supreme Court of baseball. The Commission was to include the President of each League and a third person of their choosing.

August Herrmann, Chairman of the National Commission (left), here with National League President John Heydler, was regarded by some as "Ban Johnson's boy."

This was a critical condition, because if the two League Presidents took opposing sides on an issue, the Chairman had the power to make a final decision.

In the days immediately ahead, to illustrate the point, the Commission would be faced with the ticklish chore of re-assigning the players who had jumped their contracts during the three-year war. They would decide, in other words, whether Willie Keeler belonged to Brooklyn or to the new New York Highlanders and whether Christy Mathewson should remain with the St. Louis Browns or be returned to the New York Giants.

When Johnson and Pulliam elected August Herrmann, President of the Cincinnati club, to chair the new National Commission, it looked like a victory for the National League.

But, what seems to have been unknown, overlooked or forgotten, was that Herrmann and Johnson—both Cincinnatians—were lifelong friends.

Thus, with the signing of the New National Agreement during the winter months, the wily Johnson not only achieved his major goal of achieving official recognition of the American League as a Major circuit; he also got considerable influence with the Chairman of the National Commission, now the most powerful man in baseball.

32 Little Napoleon

FOLLOWING THE WAR between the National and American leagues, baseball entered its most stable period, with club locations remaining fixed for the next 56 years. And while 1903 marked the beginning of a new era for baseball, it also signaled the rise to prominence of John McGraw.

That was the year when McGraw moved the last-place Giants of the year before to a close second behind Pittsburgh as Christy Mathewson (re-assigned to New York after the war with the American League) and Joe McGinnity won 51 games between them. The next year the Giants won their first pennant under McGraw, now only 32 years old.

In the American League, Boston won the flag but, even though the Pirates and Boston had played a lucrative post-season "World Series" in 1903 (won by Boston), McGraw and owner John Brush refused to meet the Red Sox in 1904. "Why should we play them?" McGraw snorted. "We're the real champions of the Major Leagues."

While this generated a great deal of publicity, it wasn't until 1905 that the name John McGraw began to make an indelible impression on the sporting world. For that was the year the Giants fought their way to another pennant victory and turned in one of the greatest World Series performances of all time. It was also the year in which McGraw became embroiled in a battle with an opposing manager, an umpire, a club owner and the President of the National League.

The Pirates, with an offense built around their great shortstop, Honus Wagner, turned the season into a fierce two-team race. Spicing matters up toward the end of the season, McGraw and Pirate manager Fred Clarke nearly came to blows over the merciless "riding" McGraw was giving a Pirate pitcher in a game at the Polo Grounds in New York.

Convinced that McGraw was the aggressor, the umpire ordered him off the field. Protesting all the way, McGraw removed himself to a partially hidden area behind the New York dugout.

Clarke spotted McGraw and complained to the umpire, who gave McGraw the heave-ho, this time all the way.

But matters didn't end there. In the days that followed there were these developments:

- Pirate owner Barney Dreyfuss complained to newsmen about McGraw's conduct, and McGraw responded with several uncomplimentary remarks about Dreyfuss.
- Dreyfuss filed charges with National League President, Harry Pulliam.

- McGraw blasted Pulliam for releasing the charges to the newspapers before he had a chance to defend himself. Pulliam, trying to emulate Ban Johnson's crackdown on misbehavior among players and managers, promptly fined and suspended McGraw for 15 days.
- In reviewing the squabble, the League chastised Dreyfuss, but let McGraw's fine and suspension stand.
- John Brush went to court and successfully blocked the suspension.

While all this endeared McGraw to the Giants' fans, it was the nine-game lead over second-place Pittsburgh and the outcome of the World Series that began to elevate him to the level of a demigod.

In the first "official" World Series played under uniform rules, the Giants faced Connie Mack's Philadelphia Athletics.

Christy Mathewson, who had won 32 and lost 8 during the season while compiling an earned run average of a mere 1.20, pitched against Eddie Plank in the first game of the Series and won 3 to 0. After Joe McGinnity lost by the same score in a pitching duel with Chief Bender, the As' tall Indian, Matty racked up another win opposing Andy Coakley, this time by a score of 9 to 0.

In game 4, McGinnity redeemed himself by besting Plank 1 to 0. Then, facing Bender in Game 5, Mathewson again overpowered the As as the Giants rolled to a 2 to 0 victory to end a Series that established three records that still stand. They are most complete shutouts won by a pitcher (Mathewson with three); most shutouts won by a team (Giants with four); and the most shutouts for both Series participants (five).

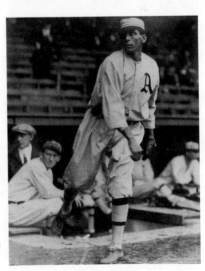

Chief Bender of the As. Shutouts in the first "official" World Series by Bender and the Giants' Christy Mathewson and Joe McGinnity set three records that still stand.

While the players did the pitching, batting and fielding, McGraw received a great deal of credit for the Giants' success. And rightly so.

This, after all, was the dead-ball era; an era in which pitchers dominated baseball and scores were low, averaging less than three earned runs a game. Whenever a team got a runner on base, the total strategy was to bring that man across the plate. That strategy did not include the long ball, or home run.

To illustrate the need to move runners by utilizing the hit-and-run, bunt and steal, one need only look at these homer records for 1905:

> Individual high, National League — 9.
> Team high, National League — 39.
> League total, National League — 182.
> Individual high, American League — 8.
> Team high, American League — 29.
> League total, American League — 155.

McGraw was a master at the one-run-at-a-time style of play; a style soon copied by others.

Once the Giants were on the field, McGraw called virtually every pitch and passed the sign for every offensive move.

An active manager until 1932, McGraw won 10 pennants and three World Series in 28 full seasons with the Giants. Only twice in that span did he finish in the second division.

Under McGraw, the Giants, like the New York Yankees in later years, became the best-known team in baseball. And McGraw, dubbed "Little Napoleon," became the best-known manager.

33 The Mythmakers

ALTHOUGH AL SPALDING and his good friend Abraham Mills occasionally disagreed, they were locked in step on one subject — the origin of baseball.

To Spalding, baseball was "the exponent of American courage, confidence, combativeness; American dash, discipline, determination; American energy, eagerness, enthusiasm; American pluck, persistency, performance; American spirit, sagacity, success; American vim, vigor, virility."

When Spalding's White Stockings and John Ward's All-Americans

John McGraw was called baseball's "Little Napoleon," and looked the part.

were feted at famed Delmonico's restaurant in New York City at the conclusion of the World Tour in 1889, Mills raised his glass and shouted, "To baseball! The American game!"

The distinguished audience, which included the Mayor of New York, a bevy of Congressmen, several U.S. Senators, the toast of Broadway and humorist Mark Twain, responded with vigorous applause and cries of "no more rounders!"

But Henry Chadwick, the dean of baseball writers and the editor of *The Spalding Baseball Guide*, demurred, insisting that baseball was nothing but "glorified rounders"; rounders being a game Chadwick played as a child in England, where he was born.

Spalding chided Chadwick about his position for years, saying that he was prejudiced in favor of rounders.

When Chadwick wrote an article for *The Guide* in 1903 upholding the rounders theory, Spalding had enough, saying he had been fed this "pap" for 40 years.

Within a year, he had rounded up a blue-ribbon committee to settle the question of baseball's origin "once and for all." The chairman of the "Special Commission" was Mills; the Secretary, James E. Sullivan, President of the New York Amateur Athletic Union and an officer of the American Sports Publishing Company, a Spalding subsidiary.

With this pair doing all the work, the Commission began its labors by asking anyone and everyone to send it any information or evidence concerning the birth of baseball.

A finding finally surfaced late in 1907, which Spalding said was the result of "...a long, thorough, painstaking investigation of all obtainable facts..."

According to the so-called facts, which were "unanimously" supported by the Commission's illustrious members, "base ball had its origin in the United States" and "...the first scheme for playing it, according to the best evidence obtainable to date, was devised by Abner Doubleday, at Cooperstown, N.Y. in 1839."

The "best evidence" turned out to be a letter written to the Commission by an 80-year-old Colorado mining engineer named Abner Graves. According to Graves, Doubleday devised the rules for the game while they were both in school in Cooperstown. Graves also said Doubleday drew a diagram of a diamond on the ground in the "Phinney lot" in Cooperstown and sketched in the positions of 11 men.

Research by reputable historians in later years, however, showed there was no link between Doubleday and baseball.

This raises a natural question: If Abner Doubleday had no connection with baseball, who was he?

Abner Doubleday, it turns out, was a graduate of West Point and the Captain of artillery who sighted the first gun to fire in defense of Ft. Sumter, which signaled the start of the Civil War. He also served in virtually every major campaign and was the General in command of the Union Army at the end of the first day of battle at Gettysburg.

Fourteen years before the Mills Commission released its report naming Doubleday as the man who invented baseball, the General died. The man in charge of the military escort that served as a guard of honor when Doubleday's body lay in state in New York's City Hall and the subsequent burial in Arlington Cemetery was none other than Abraham Mills. (Both were members of the same veterans military organization.)

Still, baseball's most authoritative voice had spoken: Cooperstown was the birthplace of baseball and Doubleday was the game's creator.

Several years after this assertion, Stephen Carlton Clark and other Cooperstown folk began to collect baseball exhibits for display in a small museum. When Clark approached baseball Commissioner Ford Frick for help, Frick came up with the idea of creating a Hall of Fame to embellish the exhibits.

In 1939, on the centennial of Doubleday's supposed invention of baseball, the National Museum and Hall of Fame was dedicated amidst much fanfare and the first 13 members—elected by the Baseball Writers

The first inductees to the National Baseball Hall of Fame included (left to right, seated) **Eddie Collins, Babe Ruth, Connie Mack and Cy Young; and** (standing) **Honus Wagner, Grover Cleveland Alexander, Tris Speaker, Napoleon Lajoie, George Sisler and Walter Johnson. Ty Cobb was conspicuously absent.**

Association in 1936—were installed. These members were Ty Cobb, Babe Ruth, Christy Mathewson, Honus Wagner, Walter Johnson, Cy Young, George Wright, Tris Speaker, John McGraw, Connie Mack, Larry Lajoie, Ban Johnson and Morgan Bulkeley.

Al Spalding, whose energetic efforts to stamp baseball as America's "national game" led to the Doubleday myth and the subsequent establishment of the Hall of Fame, was not elected until 1939. That was a year AFTER Henry Chadwick and Alexander Joy Cartwright were elected, the latter being the only man who can lay any claim to having invented baseball as we know it.

Abraham Mills, the other mythmaker, has not been elected to the hallowed Hall, as already indicated.

Each year, thousands make the trip to the beautiful village of Cooperstown to visit what has become accepted as baseball's birthplace and home. To most, it is a rewarding and enriching experience. Few, if any, seem to care that the Hall and the Museum were spawned by a myth.

34 The Most of Everything

WHEN AMERICA'S LEADING baseball writers cast their ballots for the first five inductees to the Hall of Fame, they made it clear that they regarded Tyrus Raymond Cobb as the greatest ballplayer of all time. They did so by giving him 222 of a possible 226 votes, the highest number cast for any player among those elected to the Hall in 1936.

The reason, of course, was that until then—and for more than another three decades—Cobb held more lifetime records than any other player in the game. In terms of sheer accomplishment, Ty Cobb stood alone in 1939, just as he stands alone today.

Ironically, Cobb burst upon the baseball scene in 1907, the year the Mills Commission created the myth that led to the establishment of the shrine he would enter some three decades later.

Born in Narrows, Georgia, in December 1886, Cobb was the son of a schoolmaster and state Senator, W. H. Cobb, who seems to have had a strong influence on his life.

The elder Cobb wanted Ty to become a lawyer. For a time, Cobb thought he would like to study medicine. Before the issue was resolved, Ty became interested in baseball and, despite his father's objections, signed a contract with a Minor League team in Augusta in 1904.

Like John McGraw, young Cobb was unimpressive in his debut, and was cut loose almost immediately. Terribly ashamed of himself, he broke the news to his father in a phone call from Augusta. Professor Cobb consoled Ty, then asked about his plans.

With some reluctance, Ty said he'd like to try out with a team in Anniston, Georgia. His father reportedly replied, "Go after it, but don't come home a failure!"

After successfully breaking in at Anniston, Cobb moved back to Augusta, where he had the good fortune to come under the influence of George Leidy, who helped him with his hitting, baserunning, sliding, throwing and fielding—all of the basic diamond skills Cobb would need to make it to the Majors.

Cobb, who was about 5 feet 10 inches tall and weighed only 155 pounds at the time, improved so rapidly that toward the end of the 1905 season he was picked up by the Detroit Tigers for $750.

Playing the outfield as he had at Augusta, Cobb batted .240 in 41 games. It was the only time in his 24-year career that he hit below .300.

While Cobb threw with his right hand, he batted from the left side of the plate, using an unusual split grip, the left hand two or three inches above the right. If he wanted to punch the ball through or over the infield, he would slide the right hand up to the left. If he decided to slug for extra bases, the left hand came down to the right. He also shifted his feet and his position in the batter's box constantly and rarely "dug in."

Cobb had an excellent year in 1906, batting .313 in 99 games, but it wasn't until the next season, when he played in all but four games, that fans, players and sportswriters alike began to realize a new star had been born.

For that year, 1907, the 21-year-old Cobb, now at his full height of 6 feet and 1 inch and weighing 190 pounds, led the Detroit Tigers to their first pennant and topped the American League in hits, doubles, and runs batted in, stolen bases, total bases, batting average and slugging average.

This performance is all the more remarkable when you consider that pitchers still dominated the game and that young Cobb had to face many of the game's greatest, including Addie Joss of Cleveland, Ed Walsh and Doc White of Chicago, and Eddie Plank of Philadelphia, all of whom won more than 20 games that season.

Then there was Rube Waddell, who led the League in strikeouts with 232, and Cy Young with 147. The As' Chief Bender and Eddie Plank were also among the leaders.

But, that was only the beginning. Playing a 154-game schedule on grass and half of his 24-year career in the dead-ball and spit-ball era, Cobb led all others in the following categories:

- Most hits — 4,192.
- Most games — 3,034.
- Most at-bats — 11,437.
- Most runs scored — 2,245.
- Most stolen bases — 892.
- Highest batting average — .367.
- Most total bases — 5,860.
- Most steals of home — 50.

Cobb hit .420 in 1911, 410 in 1912, .390 in 1919 and 401 in 1922 and led the American League in batting 12 times, nine in succession. After being nosed out of the title in 1916 by Tris Speaker, he went on to win it three more times in a row.

While many of these records have been shaved since the 1960s, particularly by Pete Rose (4,256 hits lifetime to Cobb's 4,191, which still ranks second) and Hank Aaron (most total bases: 6,591 to Cobb's 5,860, which still ranks second), Cobb still holds a surprising number.

It should also be noted that Rose, a marvelous and highly motivated player, appeared in 528 more games than Cobb over the same number of years. Still, Cobb collected only 65 fewer hits than Rose.

On the other hand, Cobb racked up 421 more hits than Aaron, who played 23 years, one less than Cobb.

Cobb's fantastic production of base hits led to the most important record of all, his lifetime average of .367.

Ty Cobb, breaking in with the Detroit Tigers in 1907.

That's an astonishing achievement when one considers that the Majors rarely produced anyone who can compile a .350 or higher average in one season. Cobb's base hit production averaged .367 over 24 years!

At this writing, only 179 players who were in the Majors 10 years or more have had a .300-plus batting average. Of these, only five—including Cobb—have gone over the .350 mark.

To sharpen the contrast, only two—Rogers Hornsby with .358 and Joe Jackson with .356—played in the modern era.

When discussion gets around to baseball's "greatest" player, three names generally surface: Cobb, Babe Ruth and Honus Wagner. While all comparisons are relative, the following table of statistics is revealing.

	Cobb	Ruth	Wagner
Years	24	22	21
Games	3,033	2,502	2,787
Life Batting Avg.	.367	.342	.327
Championships	12	1	8
Highest Avg.	.420	.393	.381
Runs Scored	2,245	2,174	1,736
Hits	4,192	2,873	3,415
Home Runs	118	714	101
Triples	287	136	252
Doubles	724	506	640
RBIs	1,901	2,217	1,732
Stolen Bases	892	123	732

If we disregard "years" and "games," it can be seen that Cobb topped Wagner in all of the remaining 10 categories and Ruth in all but two.

Clearly, the writers made the right choice when they selected Cobb as the most important inductee to the Hall of Fame. After all, he was—and remains—baseball's greatest ballplayer; a player who had the highest batting average of all time and a player who established the greatest number of records that begin with the word "Most."

35 Shaded

THE PENNANT RACES of 1908 were the hottest in Major League history, bringing baseball to new heights of popularity.

In the National League, the Giants, Pirates and Cubs roared to a possible three-way tie on the last day of the season. The Pirates were eliminated, however, and the Giants and Cubs were forced to replay a disputed regular-season game that had ended in a 1 to 1 tie at the Polo Grounds on September 23.

In that game, with two out in the bottom of the ninth and Moose McCormick on third as the potential winning run and rookie Fred Merkle on first, Al Bridwel rapped a low liner to right center.

When Merkle saw McCormick cross the plate as he raced for second, he did what other players had done for years in this situation; he changed course and ran to the clubhouse to avoid the hundreds of delirious Giant fans pouring out of the stands and onto the field.

In the midst of the confusion that followed, second baseman Johnny Evers got hold of a ball, stepped on second and claimed a forceout that would nullify the run.

Late that night, Evers was upheld by the umpires and the game was declared a tie. The League, however, failed to make a ruling on whether the game had to be replayed until it became obvious a season tie was possible.

To the anguish of thousands of Giants fans, the Cubs won the replay 4 to 1, even though Christy Mathewson, who was having his finest year with 35 wins against 11 losses, opposed them on the mound.

The year of the "Merkle boner," as it came to be called, saw the National League set a new attendance record of almost 3.4-million fans and top the American for the first time.

Ban Johnson's League also set a record with an attendance of more than 2.7-million. And small wonder: Cleveland, Chicago, Detroit and St. Louis were all in contention right down to the wire.

On the next to last day of the season, Boston knocked Cleveland out of the running for first place, but gave it a firm grip on second. Dramatically enough, this meant the Championship would be decided when Detroit met Chicago on the last day.

As it turns out, the White Sox were no match for Detroit in the final game as the Tigers, paced by the League's best hitter, Ty Cobb (.324), rolled over the White Sox 7 to 0.

When it was over, the winning percentages were as follows:

.588	Detroit
.584	Cleveland
.579	Chicago
.546	St. Louis

One of the big questions now raised was how Ty Cobb, who led the League in hits, doubles, triples, runs-batted-in, and batting and slugging averages, would fare in the 1908 World Series against the Cubs. After all, he had been a bust in the previous World Series, batting only .200 as the Tigers lost to the Chicago Cubs in four straight games.

The answer came quickly in the first inning of Game 1, played on a wet day in Detroit, when Cobb singled home Detroit's first run. (Typically, Cobb tried to stretch his hit into a double, but was thrown out.)

In the seventh, with Detroit trailing 5 to 1, Cobb started a three-run rally by hitting a line drive through the middle that struck the pitcher.

When the next Detroit batter singled to center, Cobb raced to third, beating the throw. Always ready to take a chance, he broke for home and scored on a ground ball to the shortstop.

In the next inning, Cobb bunted and was safe on an error. As in the seventh, Cobb sped to third on another single to center. A hurried throw to nail him went wide and Cobb scored his second run.

Although the Tigers lost the game 10 to 6 and the Series four games to one, Cobb redeemed himself by collecting seven hits—including four home runs—in 19 trips to the plate for a .368 average.

Cobb's record continued to improve in 1909. That year, as the Tigers beat back a tough Philadelphia team assembled by Connie Mack, Cobb led the League in virtually every offensive department. He batted .377, drove in 107 runs, hit nine homers, stole 76 bases and was tops in hits, slugging average, runs scored and total bases.

The Tigers' opponents in the World Series that year turned out to be the Pittsburgh Pirates, a team that finished 6 1/2 games ahead of the second place Cubs and 18 1/2 in front of third place New York.

Before the start of the 1909 World Series, Honus Wagner (left) and Ty Cobb discovered they both used the same split grip while batting, and came about it naturally.

The Series put Cobb in a matchup with the pride of the National League, Honus Wagner. Like Cobb in the American, Wagner was the offensive star in the National, batting .339 and driving in an even 100 runs as he collected his seventh League batting title.

Though the Pirates beat Detroit in a seven-game Series, neither Cobb nor Wagner turned out to be stars. But both played well.

Cobb, for example, collected six hits in 26 trips to the plate for a .231 average and drove in five runs, high for his team. He also scored two runs and stole two bases, one of which was a swipe of home that stunned the crowd in the third inning of Game 2.

Wagner, 13 years older than Cobb at 35, batted .333 and stole six bases, high for the Series.

Thus, when the two greatest players of the period met in a World Series for the first and only time, it was Cobb who had his performance shaded by a peer.

Still, by the end of his career, Ty Cobb had clearly set the standard for all-round offensive play in Major League baseball.

36 The Lone Wolf

WHILE BASEBALL people quickly became conscious of Ty Cobb's skills as a ballplayer, they also began to notice something else — his fanatical desire to excel.

Yes, fanatical.

No one before or since has ever played baseball with the intensity and driving spirit of Ty Cobb. To Cobb, baseball was not a game, it was a crusade.

From his first time at bat in the Majors, when he faced spitballer Jack Chesbro of the Highlanders and doubled in two runs, until the day he retired more than two decades later, Cobb played like a man driven by some unseen inner flame.

While it seems farfetched, some people attribute his fierce competitiveness to a family tragedy that occurred August 8, 1905, while Cobb was playing ball at Augusta. On that day, Cobb learned that his mother had blown his father's brains out with a double-barreled shotgun.

Apparently W. H. Cobb had suspected his wife of infidelity and, after leaving her home alone, had returned to spy on her as she prepared for bed. Since it was dark and late at night, Mrs. Cobb became frightened when she saw a dark figure trying to open the bedroom window. Instinctively, she picked up a shotgun that always stood in the corner and fired two blasts at the intruder.

Only after neighbors came to investigate did she learn that she had killed her husband.

After a coroner's hearing the next day, Mrs. Cobb was arrested on a manslaughter charge. A year later, she was tried and acquitted.

Whether or not the grisly incident affected Cobb's personality is open to conjecture. He did say later that the day of the shooting was the "blackest day of my life."

Whatever the reason behind Cobb's driving spirit, he became an aggressive, combative, tough, ruthless, fearless and unrelenting ballplayer.

When Cobb ran the bases, he took the view — and correctly so — that the paths belonged to him. If someone got in the way and was cut by his high-flying spikes — as they often were — that was their fault.

At bat, the pitcher was his enemy and every pitch meant an opportunity to destroy that enemy.

Pitchers who dared throw at Cobb could expect him to bunt down the first base line. When they tried to field the ball they would do so at great risk, since Cobb would deliberately run up and over them, knees and spikes churning.

This slide into "Home Run" Baker by Ty Cobb sparked death threats.

Cobb was just as ruthless when he found a player between him and second or third base, or home plate.

He was on first one day in a game against the Washington Senators, for instance, when Harry Heilmann singled to right field. As usual, Cobb tore around second and headed for third.

The throw to third baseman Ossie Bluege had him beat by several feet. Bluege moved out to meet Cobb and make the tag.

Instead of trying to elude Bluege, Cobb left the ground, flew through the air spikes first and crashed into the third-sacker like a battering ram. The "slide" was so obviously an attempt to maim Bluege that Cobb was tossed out of the game.

The next day Cobb apologized to Bluege and said he hoped he wasn't hurt. In the next breath, however, he issued a warning: "Never come up the line to meet me."

In a somewhat similar situation in Detroit, Cobb spiked the Philadelphia As' popular third baseman, Frank "Home Run" Baker, cutting Baker's upper arm slightly.

Connie Mack and the A's complained bitterly, but news pictures showed that Baker had reached across the bag with his bare hand to tag Cobb and the spiking could not have been deliberate.

Still, when Detroit arrived in Philadelphia a few weeks later, Cobb received several threatening letters, one of which promised that if he dared play against the A's "you will be shot from one of the buildings outside the park."

Ty Cobb was not the fastest baserunner in the game while he was playing, but he was certainly the most daring. Going from first to third on a bunt was almost routine. And, quite often, he would score from first on a single.

As for stealing bases, no one came close to him in this department. On four occasions (still a record) he stole second, third and home. (It should be remembered that of all the individual offensive maneuvers, stealing home is the rarest and most difficult.)

In the entire history of the game, only 37 players have notched more than ten steals of home. Of these, Max Carey is closest to Cobb's record of 50 with 33.

Cobb's presence at bat or on the basepaths was a tremendous asset to his team because it put a great deal of pressure on every defensive player. Such pressure, of course, often causes players to make mistakes — dropped balls, overthrows, wild pitches, balks or collisions in the outfield. Defensive mistakes also mean giving up extra bases and runs and, quite often, allowing an additional player to come to the plate.

This, then, was Cobb's modus operandi. This was his game.

And while Cobb starred on offense, he was also an excellent outfielder. He studied the opposing batters and got to know their strengths and weaknesses. By the same token, he knew what kind of pitch to expect from the Tigers staff in almost every situation. This meant that he was usually in the right spot when the ball was hit to the area he was assigned to defend. In one game, in fact, he threw three men out at first on clean singles!

Even though Cobb didn't drink or smoke during his playing days and took good care of his body, he paid a high price physically for his slashing, aggressive style of play.

The great sportswriter, Grantland Rice, wrote that he once visited Cobb in his hotel room before a game against the Yankees. He said Cobb had a high temperature and a heavy cold and that his legs were "a mass of raw flesh and adhesive."

"You had to have a strong stomach to look at them," Rice reported.

That afternoon Cobb had three hits and stole two bases, sliding each time.

Sadly, Cobb had few friends on the diamond or off. For most of his life, despite his enormous ability as a ballplayer and great wealth accumulated through prudent investments, Ty Cobb was, in effect, a lone wolf.

37 The Czar

THE AMERICAN LEAGUE owners' confidence in Ban Johnson was such that in 1910 they re-elected him to a 20-year term with a substantial increase in pay. And since he and his friend August Herrmann represented two-thirds of baseball's three-man Supreme Court, he continued to have the upper hand in matters affecting both the Major and Minor Leagues.

Most of all, he dominated affairs in his own circuit, where he relentlessly pursued and/or prosecuted anyone suspected or found guilty of acts reflecting on the integrity of the game.

Inevitably, his autocratic rule brought him into situations involving the mercurial Ty Cobb.

For most of his career, Cobb was notorious for his fist fights on and off the diamond. His pugilistic encounters in the Big League began when he joined the Tigers. And they started with his own teammates, several of whom formed a clique that tried to drive him off the club.

The group harassed Cobb in several ways. It began by ostracizing anyone who tried to room with him, or was friendly with him. The members of the clique also sawed in half several of his favorite bats; bats he made himself back home in Royston.

Some of the hazing heaped on Cobb was, of course, normal treatment for a rookie and regarded by the older players as "fun." But Cobb was deadly serious about his work and showed little sense of humor about anything. He refused to take any abuse, no matter how slight, from the Tigers or anyone else. On the road, he ate alone and lived alone. And he took life so seriously that he began to go to bed with a loaded pistol under his pillow.

Fighting in the Tiger clubhouse became so constant during Cobb's early years with Detroit that manager Hughie Jennings tried to trade him to Cleveland for Elmer Flick.

Cobb also had his problems off the field. In Cleveland, in 1909, he got into an argument with the black elevator operator in his hotel and slapped the man. A black night watchman came to the elevator operator's defense. As the two argued, Cobb pulled a knife, the watchman countered by pulling a gun and clubbing Cobb over the head with his nightstick.

Whenever Cobb stepped on the diamond in Detroit, the hometown crowd came roaring to its feet, applauding and cheering his every move. The fans also jumped to their feet when he appeared on the field in other cities. Mostly, however, he was the target of derisive hoots and howls of hate and vituperation, a reaction that not only failed to intimidate Cobb, but goaded him to greater efforts.

Ban Johnson, baseball's first "Czar."

One of those who took great delight in heaping verbal abuse on Cobb was a New York Highlander fan named Claude Lueker, who somehow had lost one hand and part of another. Lueker, with a voice like a foghorn, often sat near the Tiger bench whenever Detroit visited New York. Cobb was Lueker's target, and he blasted out insults and barbs that could be heard clear across the field.

One day Lueker called out that Cobb was "half nigger," the ultimate insult to a Southerner of Cobb's upbringing and background. Ignoring the possibility that he could be mobbed and badly beaten, Cobb threw down his glove, jumped into the seats and battered Lueker about the head and body with his fists.

Angry fans around Lueker called out to Cobb that Lueker had "no hands."

"I don't care if he has no feet!" was Cobb's response as he pounded Lueker.

Pulled away by park police, the outfielder clawed and shoved his way back to the field where several of his teammates were gathered at the sideline, each holding a bat that was clearly meant to dent a few skulls.

While Cobb was thumbed out of the game, his unprecedented act, witnessed by Ban Johnson, brought a swift suspension.

Matters didn't end there, however, for Cobb's teammates defied Johnson. They sent him a telegram saying they wouldn't play for the Tigers again until the suspension was lifted.

If the Tigers didn't field a team against the As, the club would have to pay a $5,000 forfeiture fee imposed by Johnson's office.

Manager Jennings begged his players to relent, but they refused.

To avoid the fee, Jennings rounded up several Philadelphia college players and semi-pros to fill the ranks of the strikers. (They were easily beaten by the As, 24 to 2.)

The players' strike was, of course, the kind of challenge Johnson loved. He fined each man who signed the telegram of protest $100 and threatened to bar all involved from the game for life. After looking at the umpire's report, Johnson then set Cobb's suspension at 10 days and fined him $50.

At Cobb's urging, the players ended their strike before the next scheduled game. When they did, Ban Johnson had scored the kind of victory that earned him a title: "The Czar of Baseball."

38 Enter the Judge

NOT LONG AFTER Ban Johnson cracked down on the Tigers for their one-day strike, there were rumors that the Federal League, a Minor loop founded in 1913, might try to convert to a Major the following year.

The rumors became fact when four wealthy and powerful industrialists threw their money and weight behind the Federals. They included Robert B. Ward, Ward Baking Co.; Harry F. Sinclair, Sinclair Oil; Charles Weeghman of Chicago, owner of a chain of restaurants; and Philip Ball of St. Louis, a manufacturer of ice-making equipment.

The money-laden owners were successful in getting Three-Finger Brown, Joe Tinker and other prominent players to join the Federals. Hefty offers were also made to John McGraw, Ty Cobb and Walter Johnson, but those stars remained where they were.

Astonishingly, the Federals were operating fully in 1914, and several of the clubs were in new parks.

The franchise lineup as the season got underway looked like this.

National League	American League	Federal League
Chicago	Chicago	Chicago
St. Louis	St. Louis	St. Louis
Pittsburgh	Philadelphia	Pittsburgh
Boston	Boston	Indianapolis
New York	New York	Baltimore
Brooklyn	Washington	Brooklyn
Philadelphia	Detroit	Buffalo
Cincinnati	Cleveland	Kansas City

As usual, the spectacle of players jumping from one team to another began to adversely affect attendance, and before the end of the second year, all three Leagues were losing money. The three Leagues were also losing a great deal of time, money and effort suing each other in the courts, mostly in an effort to keep control of players.

The most important suit was filed by the Federals in the U.S. District Court in Chicago against Organized Baseball, the 16 Presidents of the National and American League clubs and the National Commission.

The suit, which charged the defendants with violation of the Sherman Anti-Trust Act, asked the Court to take the following steps:

- Declare the National Agreement illegal.
- Avoid all acts of the National Commission.
- Nullify all contracts made under the National Agreement.
- Dismiss all suits brought against the Federal League by Organized Baseball.

Obviously, the suit was aimed at the heart of professional baseball. If the Federals won, the structure of the game would be destroyed.

The judge presiding over the case made some comments, however, that gave the American and National leagues considerable heart.

"Do you realize a decision in this case may tear down the very foundations of the game, so beloved by thousands?" the judge asked the lawyers facing him.

He then went on to observe that both sides should understand "that any blow to the thing called baseball would be regarded by this court as a blow to a national institution."

Still, the Federals pushed for a decision in the case. On the other side, only Ban Johnson favored a decision because he believed the critical reserve clause would be upheld.

But the judge refused to rule, making it clear he hoped the parties would get together and settle. In the winter of 1916, just when the

Federals were threatening to move a team into the most lucrative area, New York City, and it seemed as if the war would go on forever, a National League committee met secretly with representatives of the Federal League and worked out a peace agreement.

Pittsburgh's Barney Dreyfuss, a member of the committee, was dispatched to Chicago to lay the details before the American League. Dreyfuss, however, met vigorous opposition from Ban Johnson, who insisted the Federals were beaten. Ultimately, the American League owners refused to support Johnson's position, something they rarely, if ever, had done up to that time.

As a result, on December 21, 1915, the peace treaty was entered into by the three Leagues and soon after, the lawsuit was dropped.

Under the agreement's terms, the Federals' Charles Wheegam purchased a controlling interest in the Chicago Cubs, while Phil Ball gained control of the St. Louis Browns.

The agreement also provided for reinstatement of players who jumped their contracts and put other Federal League players up for sale to the highest bidder.

When it was over, several of the owners recognized that they would never have been able to extricate themselves from the conflict with the Federal League if it hadn't been for the judge in Chicago's U.S. District Court.

His name, of course, was Kenesaw Mountain Landis. In time, it became a name baseball would never forget.

39 The Czar Falls

L IKE WILLIAM HULBERT before him, Ban Johnson's major objective was to keep baseball—especially in the American League—honest, profitable and above reproach. These were worthy goals, to be sure.

During his long and autocratic reign, however, Johnson stepped on a lot of toes. But as long as he had the support of the American League owners, it didn't seem to matter. He could defy the players, the public and the press. In effect, he could rule with impunity. And he did.

Suprisingly, the first serious challenge to Johnson's rule as baseball's "Czar" came from the National League and involved the assignment of a brilliant young player named George Sisler.

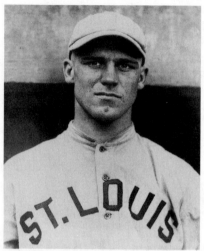

A dispute over who owned George
Sisler rocked baseball's inner circle.

Pittsburgh owner Barney Dreyfuss
launched a campaign to dissolve the
National Commission and replace it
with a single ruler.

Sisler was signed by Branch Rickey, General Manager of the St. Louis Browns, when Sisler graduated from the University of Michigan in 1915. But when Sisler was 17 years old and in high school, he had signed a contract to play with Akron, a Minor League club.

Although Sisler never played for Akron, or any other professional club, his contract—or title—was eventually sold to the Pittsburgh Pirates.

Since Sisler was a great performer, Pittsburgh wanted him and took the matter before the three-man National Commission, which consisted of Johnson, Garry Herrmann and a new President of the National League, John Tener, a former Governor of Pennsylvania.

Johnson, of course, voted in favor of the Browns and, as usual, Herrmann sided with him.

During the winter meetings that year, Dreyfuss began a campaign to get rid of the three-man Commission because, he said, "Garry is Ban's boy."

Dreyfuss advocated that the Commission be replaced with a single person not directly involved with baseball; his plan didn't get much support until the culmination of a series of events that began in 1918.

That year, Charles Comiskey signed pitcher Jack Quinn after the Pacific Coast League disbanded in midseason. After Quinn won five

The decision about who owned pitcher Jack Quinn ended Ban Johnson's long friendship with Charles Comiskey.

Charles Comiskey, owner of the Chicago White Sox.

games for Chicago, the New York Yankees purchased his release from his former club.

When the dispute over ownership of the pitcher was laid before Johnson, he ruled in favor of the Yankees. That decision brought an end to Johnson's friendship with Comiskey, a friendship that had lasted more than 25 years.

In still another dispute that year, the Boston Braves claimed ownership of Scott Perry, a pitcher with the Philadelphia Athletics.

Johnson, as expected, voted for Philadelphia, but this time, Herrmann sided with John Tener and ordered Perry to report to the National League Boston club.

Unlike Dreyfuss, who accepted the Commission's ruling, Connie Mack and owner Ben Shibe went to court and were successful in retaining Perry.

Tener, suspecting that Johnson encouraged the As to take court action, urged his owners to break off relations with the American League.

The National Leaguers refused to do so because they were reluctant to give up the World Series. As a result, Tener resigned in anger and was replaced by John Heydler.

Just before the winter meetings, sports pages predicted that Garry Herrmann would not be re-elected Chairman of the National Commission.

Although Johnson managed to corral enough votes to retain Herrmann, his power eroded rapidly in 1919 when he tried to nullify a deal the Yankeees made for Carl Mays, a Boston Red Sox pitcher who had won 21 games the year before.

Mays, unhappy by the kind of support he was getting from his fielders, had walked out on the Sox during a midseason game with Chicago. A short time later, Red Sox owner Harry Frazee sold the pitcher to the New York Yankees for $40,000 and two players.

Because Mays had broken his contract, Johnson suspended the right-handed submarine-ball pitcher and told his umpires not to allow Mays on the diamond in a New York uniform.

Colonel Tillinghast Huston and Colonel Jacob Ruppert, owners of the New York Yankees, went to court and won.

In retaliation, Johnson ruled that eight games won by Mays while pitching for the Yankees were invalid. This meant that the Yankees were to be dropped from third to fourth place in the standings and their players would lose the third place share of the World Series gate.

This so angered the anti-Johnson faction—Comiskey, Frazee, Ruppert and Huston—there was talk of pulling out of the American League and joining the National to form another 12-team circuit.

That winter, however, the League Presidents voted to award Mays to the Yankees and restore the third place World Series money. Later, when Garry Herrmann realized he couldn't win re-election, he resigned from the Commission.

The two Leagues next ordered John Heydler and Johnson to find a new Chairman—someone who had no financial interest in baseball.

Clearly, the Czar had fallen from power.

40 A New Hero

FROM ITS VERY inception, baseball has been a changing game.
Generally, changes were introduced gradually, so gradually that they were often hardly noticed. But in 1919, the biggest, swiftest and most dramatic change in baseball history was brought about by a big moon-faced pitcher/outfielder named George Herman "Babe" Ruth, a player who was so strong he swung a 54-ounce bat.

That year, Ruth did what no one had done before him: he hit an astonishing 29 home runs, two more than the record set by Ed Williamson in 1844. For the season, he more than doubled the homer output of any other player in the Majors.

Ruth began playing baseball in St. Mary's Industrial Home for Boys in Baltimore. He first entered the school in 1902 when he was almost 9 years old. Ruth's father, who ran a saloon in Baltimore, and his mother, who was often ill, had difficulty getting Ruth to go to school and put him in St. Mary's as an "incorrigible."

Ruth excelled in all sports and first began playing baseball as a catcher, even though he was left-handed. At about 17, however, he began to pitch.

Jack Dunn, Manager of the Baltimore Orioles, then a Minor League team, heard about Ruth's prowess as a pitcher and took a look at him. Dunn liked what he saw and, after agreeing to become Ruth's guardian until he was 21, signed the young hurler just before the 1914 season for $600, or $100 a month for six months. Ruth had just passed his 20th birthday.

Because he constantly followed Dunn about the Orioles training camp in Fayetteville, North Carolina, that spring, Ruth was referred to by the older players as Dunn's "new babe." From then on, it was Babe Ruth, destined to be the most famous name in baseball.

Ruth didn't stay with the Orioles long. The team was strapped for money because many fans had switched allegiance to the city's Federal League team. Ultimately, Dunn had to sell Ruth to the Boston Red Sox shortly after the season opened in a package deal that included another pitcher, Ernie Shore, and an infielder. The price tag was $22,000.

Appearing in five games after he joined the Red Sox, Ruth hurled 23 innings and got credit for two wins and one loss. He also pitched three innings in relief without a decision. In 10 times at bat, he collected two hits, one of them a double.

While Ruth was impressive, manager Bill 'Rough' Carrigan thought he needed more experience and farmed him out to Providence in the International League.

A week before the Major League season ended, Ruth was recalled by the Red Sox, marking the last time he would ever play in the Minors during a career that lasted 22 years.

In 1915, Ruth began in earnest what appeared to be a great pitching career. Ruth and Ernie Shore each won 18 and lost 8 as the Red Sox won the pennant, nosing out the Detroit Tigers by 2 1/2 games.

Ruth's only appearance in the World Series was as a pinch hitter in the ninth inning of the first game. He grounded out to first with one man on.

Over the next two years, Ruth continued to shine as a pitcher. In 1916, for example, he won 23 and lost 12 as the Red Sox drove to another

Babe Ruth as a pitcher for the Boston Red Sox.

pennant. Ruth's total wins that year put him second to the great Walter Johnson, who won 25. But he had the lowest earned run average in the League, with a 1.75.

He sparkled in the 1916 World Series, too. Starting the second game in Boston against the Brooklyn Dodgers, Ruth beat Sherry Smith 2 to 1 in a pitching duel that went 14 innings, setting a World Series record.

While he won 24 and lost 13 in 1917, Ruth began to establish a different kind of career the following season when the Red Sox lost several key players to military service and manager Ed Barrow was forced to use Ruth in the infield and outfield. Playing 59 games in left field and 13 at first base, Ruth batted a respectable .300 and in doing so racked up 26 doubles, 11 triples and 11 homers, which tied him for the League lead in round-trippers with Tilly Walker.

On the mound, he won 13 and lost 7 as Boston won the pennant again.

When the World Series with the Chicago Cubs rolled around, Barrow called on Ruth to hurl the opener. He won 1 to 0, going the distance.

In Game 4, with the Sox leading two games to one, Ruth again got the nod from Barrow. He tripled in two runs in the fourth, but gave up tying runs in the eighth. At this point, he had set another World Series record by shutting out his opponents for 29 2/3 innings.

With the Red Sox ahead 3 to 2 in the ninth, Ruth gave way to Joe Bush, who saved the game.

Carl Mays, winner of Game 2, pitched the Red Sox to World Series victory in Game 6 with a three-hit performance.

With the start of the 1919 season, Ruth insisted that he couldn't both pitch and play the outfield and said he would prefer to play every day. Signing after a brief holdout, he underscored his stand in spring training by hitting the original tape-measure homer. It carried well over 500 feet (Ed Barrow insisted it was 579).

When the season ended, Ruth had played 111 games in the outfield, four at first base, and appeared as a pitcher 17 times (9–5). By now, his batting and the publicity it generated—which drew huge crowds wherever he went—made Ruth a hot property.

In an unusual deal, the Yankees' Jake Ruppert paid Red Sox owner Harry Frazee $125,000 for Ruth, loaned him another $350,000 and took a mortgage on the Red Sox' Fenway Park.

But the Yankees got their money back. And then some. For the next year, 1920, Ruth, as a regular outfielder, banged out a phenomenal 58 homers, which more than tripled the homer output of any other player in the Majors. It also set a mark no one believed would ever be topped.

Overnight, Babe Ruth became a new national sports hero.

41 The Great Compromise

J UST A FEW DAYS before the 1920 season ended and a World Series shaped up between the Indians and the Brooklyn Dodgers, the worst scandal in sports history exploded in Chicago.

There, a Cook County grand jury indicted eight members of the Chicago White Sox for conspiring with gamblers to throw the "best-of-nine" 1919 World Series with the Cincinnati Reds.

The eight players included outfielder "Shoeless Joe" Jackson; spitballer Eddie "Shine Ball" Cicotte; Claude "Lefty" Williams, another pitcher; center fielder Oscar "Happy" Felsh; Charles "Swede" Risberg; first baseman Arnold "Chic" Gandil; third baseman George "Buck" Weaver and Fred McMullin, a utility infielder.

Along with second baseman Eddie Collins and catcher Ray Shalk, these players comprised one of the greatest teams ever assembled by Charles Comiskey.

In the days approaching the 1919 Series, Chicago was a clear favorite to beat the Reds. The night before the first game, however, betting suddenly shifted and the Reds became heavy favorites.

Still, it was not until the White Sox lost the first game 9 to 0 that anyone suspected the worst.

After the game, Chicago manager Kid Gleason went to Comiskey and reported that, while he had no proof, he thought gamblers had reached a few of his players. He pointed out that Cicotte, who had won 29 and lost 7, had his worst performance of the year. He also noted that several plays that afternoon were badly handled.

Comiskey, also suspicious, needed no more urging.

Under normal circumstances, Comiskey would have gone to Ban Johnson, the President of his League. But such a move posed this political dilemma:

- Comiskey and Johnson were now open enemies and not speaking to each other.
- Johnson and Heydler still had not agreed on a new Chairman for the National Commission, even though they had been directed to do so almost a year earlier. (Heydler had pushed for the appointment of Judge Landis, but Johnson had said he would have no part of the jurist because he was nothing more than "a showboat.")

As a result, Comiskey felt he had no choice but to go to the President of the rival League.

Although Heydler discounted the possibility of a "fix," he took no chances; he called Johnson.

Johnson listened to Heydler, then commented that Comiskey was trying to alibi his team's loss and that the White Sox owner's suspicions were nothing more than "the cry of a whipped cur."

For the moment, the issue was closed.

When Chicago lost the Series five games to three, however, rumors persisted that the Series had, indeed, been fixed.

For his part, Comiskey offered a $10,000 reward for evidence that would lead to conviction of any "fixers."

Johnson, with the assistance of private detectives, dug into the case with the diligence of a bloodhound. For almost a year, he interviewed gamblers, players and bookmakers all over the baseball map and even tracked a key witness to Mexico and persuaded him to testify.

Late in September of 1920, in the hope of collecting Comiskey's

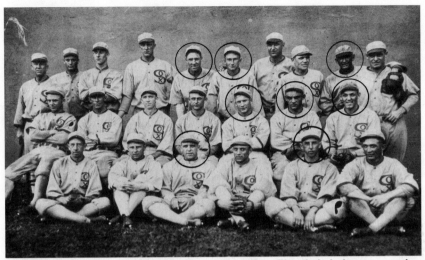

This team became known as the Chicago Black Sox. The circled players were involved in corruption charges. (Bottom row, left to right) **Eddie Cicotte and Claude Williams;** (middle row, left to right) **Happy Felsch, Chic Gandil and Buck Weaver;** (top row, left to right) **Swede Risberg, Fred McMullin and Joe Jackson. Manager Kid Gleason is the first man in the top row.**

$10,000 reward, a Philadelphia gambler named Bill Maharg told a newspaperman about his involvement in the conspiracy and implicated the eight players.

When the story broke, Cicotte went to Gleason and Comiskey and confessed. They, in turn, persuaded him to go before the Grand Jury, which had been called to investigate a game between the Chicago Cubs and the Phillies on July 20 of that year (1920). Not long afterward, Joe Jackson and Lefty Williams also confessed.

When the indictments were handed down, the 1920 White Sox were leading the League by one game with three games to play. A sorrowful Comiskey promptly suspended the eight players; and when the season ended, Cleveland finished two games ahead of Chicago, a team that would be forever known as the "Black Sox."

While most of the public attention was centered on the 1919 Series, the grand jury also turned up evidence that made it clear the fixing of games had taken place during the regular season.

The wave of publicity that followed these developments rocked baseball to its foundations and convinced panicky, frightened club owners and League officials that something had to be done to restore the game's integrity.

Albert D. Lasker, a Chicago Cubs stockholder, suggested that the Na-

Kenesaw Mountain Landis.

tional Commission be replaced by a three-man board composed of individuals who were not connected in any way with baseball.

While this idea had the support of the National League, it was favored by only three American Leaguers: the trio that opposed Johnson in the Carl Mays case — Comiskey, Ruppert of the Yankees and Frazee of the Red Sox.

To put some teeth into their proposal, the pro-Lasker group demanded that the five American League clubs still supporting Johnson get in line and approve the plan by November 1. If not, this faction threatened to add another franchise and go with a 12-team circuit in 1921.

When the November 1 deadline passed without agreement, the pro-Lasker group went ahead with its plans for a 12-team loop, referred to as "The New National League." In doing so, it voted to put the future of baseball into the hands of Judge Landis and two others.

Shortly afterward, however, the club owners of both Leagues got together in Chicago. Deliberately, they excluded League Presidents Heydler and Johnson from their meeting.

Determined to avoid another costly war, the owners agreed to continue with two eight-team leagues. And in what was probably the most important compromise in baseball history, they agreed — unanimously — that baseball should be governed by one man, Kenesaw Mountain Landis.

42 Round One

EVEN HIS ENEMIES conceded that if Ban Johnson was anything, he was a fighter. And that characteristic was never made more evident than during the sorry, tangled aftermath of the Cook County grand jury investigation of gambling in baseball and the subsequent Black Sox scandal.

In building his case, the District Attorney, with Johnson's help, had brought more than a score of witnesses before the grand jury, including players, gamblers, managers, owners and sportswriters.

One of these was Arnold Rothstein, a New York gambler and prominent member of the underworld. Rothstein, accused of being the "mastermind" of the plot, was said to have agreed to give the players $100,000 to lose the Series; $20,000 before each game.

While the truth may never be known about Rothstein's role and the role of others in the bizarre case, here are the main points of the story told by gambler Billy Maharg:

- Sleepy Bill Burns, a pitcher who spent five unimpressive years in the Majors and left the game in 1912, introduced Maharg to Eddie Cicotte and Chic Gandil in a New York hotel after a game with the Yankees. There, the players agreed to "fix" the Series for $100,000.
- Maharg and Burns offered the deal to Rothstein. Rothstein declined.
- Several days later, Maharg told Burns he had met Abe Attel, a former featherweight champion, who told him that Rothstein had changed his mind and would now finance the fix, with Attel handling the cash.
- On the morning of Game 1, Burns and Maharg met Attel in a Cincinnati hotel room and asked for the money. Attel said he needed the money to bet, but would make a payoff after each game that was lost. Attel reneged on the first loss.
- After the second game was lost, Maharg and Burns again went to Attel. This time, he gave them $10,000. According to this story, that was all the players ever received.

Rothstein offered a different tale when he appeared before the grand jury. He said it was Attel and Burns who had approached him for the $100,000 needed to ensure that the White Sox would lose. He claimed he spurned the offer because he didn't believe it was possible to fix a World Series. He added that he had bet $6,000 on the White Sox.

While differing versions of what happened and who got what appeared years later, it was the Maharg story that triggered the indictments in September 1920.

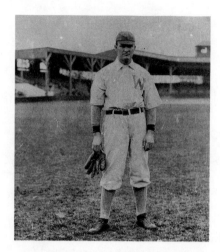

Sleepy Bill Burns tried to hide in Mexico.

In October, the grand jury exonerated Rothstein.

A month later, a new prosecuting attorney took office in Chicago. When he set out to prepare the Black Sox case for trial, he was astonished to discover that the signed confessions of Jackson, Cicotte and Williams and all other related evidence had disappeared from the files. In relating this to Ban Johnson, he said, "Nothing's left but the paper on the wall."

This meant that if the conspirators were to be tried, new evidence had to be found by April of the following year (1921) to comply with the law.

After Johnson reported this to Commissioner Landis, the first and only boss he'd ever had in more than two decades in baseball, he wanted to know what Landis proposed to do about the situation.

Landis directed some threatening remarks at the unknown individuals who had stolen the evidence, but it was clear he was adopting a wait-and-see posture.

Angered by this, Johnson decided to take matters into his own hands.

Over the next several months, he traveled back and forth across the country gathering evidence to re-indict the Chicago players. He even tracked Sleepy Bill Burns to Mexico and persuaded the former pitcher and key witness in the case to return to Chicago and testify.

In a strange twist to the case, in the meantime, an unidentified individual offered to sell the stolen evidence to a newspaper for $25,000. (The paper turned the offer down when it learned of the theft.)

Shortly thereafter, Johnson issued a statement saying that Arnold Rothstein had paid someone $15,000 to steal the evidence. He said Rothstein wanted to learn what he, Johnson, had told the grand jury

Featherweight Champion Abe Attel, a treacherous go-between.

about a meeting they had had in New York several weeks before the original indictments were returned.

Rothstein immediately denied the accusation and announced he was filing a $500,000 libel action against Johnson.

Typically, the fiery Johnson said he hoped the suit would be forthcoming so the courts could get at the truth of the matter.

Rothstein, however, failed to follow through on his threat. (He was murdered several years later.)

By the summer of 1921, the District Attorney felt he had enough evidence to finally bring the players and five gamblers to trial on a charge of criminal conspiracy.

Without the signed confessions, however, the case proved to be too weak; after it was presented, a jury brought in a verdict of "not guilty."

When those two words were spoken, they set off a wild celebration in the courtroom among the defendants and their supporters.

Above the cries of jubilation, Chic Gandil was heard to say, "To hell with Ban Johnson!" He followed that up with this comment: "I guess that will learn Ban Johnson that he can't frame an honest bunch of players."

That night, the players and many of the jurors partied at a Chicago restaurant into the early hours of the morning. (Today, because the players as a group were extraordinarily close-mouthed and took their versions of the facts about their involvement in the scandal to their graves, several questions remain unanswered.)

While Commissioner Landis remained in the wings during the second investigation of the Black Sox scandal, he stepped to center stage when it was over and barred the eight players from baseball for life. In doing so, he issued this ringing statement: "Regardless of the verdict of juries, no player who throws a ballgame, no player who entertains proposals or promises to throw a game, no player who sits in a conference with a bunch of crooked players and does not promptly tell his club about it, will ever again play professional baseball. . . ."

With the acquittal of the eight players, Ban Johnson had lost his toughest fight in baseball. As to his new relationship with Commissioner Landis, it was only Round 1.

43 One of a Kind

T HROUGHOUT ITS LONG LIFE, baseball has been crowded with colorful characters. But it has never seen anyone quite like Kenesaw Mountain Landis.

A short, slightly built string bean of a man, Landis had large, dark, brooding eyes that were deeply set in a thin-lipped, craggy face that seemed to be fixed in a perpetual scowl. By the time Landis became Commissioner of Baseball, his thick, wavy hair had become pure white, a feature that served to enhance the burning eyes.

He always wore a high, starched collar and baggy, rumpled suits. When he wore a hat, it was usually a soft fedora with a wide, floppy brim and a high, oddly dented, shapeless crown.

Thus, despite his lack of size, Landis was a man who attracted immediate attention wherever he went and whenever he spoke. Landis loved the attention he received and played his role of the Important Man to the hilt. He was, as Ban Johnson said, a showboat.

Landis was the sixth of seven children born to Dr. Abraham Landis and Mary Kulmer Landis. His birthplace was Millville, Ohio and his birthdate November 20, 1866.

His father apparently christened him Kenesaw Mountain as a reminder of his experiences in the Civil War. While serving as a surgeon in the Union Army, Dr. Landis lost a leg during an engagement with Confederate forces on Kennesaw Mountain in Georgia. For some unknown reason, one "n" was dropped from the boy's first name.

When Landis was 7 or 8 years old, the family moved to a small farm in northwestern Indiana; that's where he spent most of his youth.

Ken Landis delivered newspapers as a boy and loved to play baseball but became interested in law at an early age. After teaching himself shorthand, he landed a job as a court stenographer in his home county.

Though he did not have a formal college education, Landis completed law courses at the Y.M.C.A. Law School of Cincinnati, obtained a law degree from Chicago's Union Law School and was admitted to the bar in Illinois in 1891.

Fourteen years later President Theodore Roosevelt appointed him to the Federal bench in the court for the Northern District, the same court in which Landis heard the suit filed by the Federal League against Organized Baseball.

During his stay on the bench, Judge Landis ruled on several cases that gained considerable attention, the most celebrated of which involved the Standard Oil Company.

It was alleged that when the oil company shipped oil via the Chicago and Alton Railroad, it accepted rebates for each carload, a violation of law. Landis created a stir by calling John D. Rockfeller, Sr., to court to testify about the charges.

At the conclusion of the case, Standard Oil was found guilty and Landis imposed a fine of $29.2-million. Although reversed by the U.S. Supreme Court, Landis was for years identified as "the man who fined Standard Oil over $29-million."

Irascible, stubborn, prejudiced, strong-willed and tart, Landis was a man one either loved or hated.

Baseball's owners got a quick taste of the Landis character that historic day in November 1920 when they voted to hire him at $50,000 a year to "save" the game.

After Landis was elected, the Presidents of the 16 clubs rushed to his court to break the news to the Judge. When they got there, however, Landis ignored them and continued to hear a case going on before him. At one point, he even scolded the owners for making too much noise.

Later, when all were finally invited to join him in his chambers, he coldly and blithely inquired, "Gentlemen, what is the purpose of your visit?"

After it was explained that the owners were there to offer him the job of Baseball Commissioner, Landis was hesitant. He said he was doing "important work" and wasn't sure he should give it up.

The stunned owners couldn't believe their ears.

Finally it was suggested that perhaps he could do both jobs: stay on the bench and rule baseball.

After mulling it over, the Judge decided that was a good idea. Still, he didn't accept until assured he would have full control of the game.

He then brought up one more point: He said he would subtract his

Judge Landis (second from left) **is seen here with some of the owners who put the fate of their ballclubs in his hands. They include** (left to right) **Jake Ruppert and Tillinghast Huston of the Yankees and Harry Frazee of the Boston Red Sox. The fifth man in the picture could not be identified.**

$7,500 Federal Government salary from the $50,000 baseball would pay him.

With a sigh of relief, the owners murmured their agreement. After hands were shaken all around, the Judge issued a statement to the press.

"I have accepted the chairmanship of baseball on the invitation of the 16 major league clubs," he said. "At their request and in accordance with my own earnest wishes I am to remain on the bench and continue my work here. The opportunities for real service are limitless. It is a matter to which I have been devoted for nearly 40 years. On the question of policy, all I have to say is this:

"The only thing in anybody's mind now is to make and keep baseball what the millions of fans throughout the United States want it to be."

When the owners decided on Landis in the November meeting, they also agreed to appoint a committee to rewrite the National Agreement to accommodate the change in leadership. The agreement, signed two months after Landis' appointment, gave the judge extraordinary power for a period of 25 years. It enabled him, for example, to investigate virtually anything construed to be detrimental to the interests of baseball.

If he chose to do so, he could fine anyone connected with the game as much as $5,000. He also had the power to suspend, reprimand or—as in the case of the Black Sox—bar anyone from the game who was deemed to have been guilty of a transgression.

What's more, the agreement denied owners the right to overrule or set aside a Landis decision, or take the Judge to court in any disagreement.

From that point on, owners, players and fans alike came to learn that Judge Kenesaw Mountain Landis was one of a kind.

44 The Lesson

THE INK WAS hardly dry on his contract when Commissioner Kenesaw Mountain Landis launched a series of decisions in 1921 that clearly spelled out how he intended to rule over his new domain, Organized Baseball.

His first case was one that Ban Johnson and John Heydler, the two league presidents, had failed to settle before he took office. It involved the ownership of a pitcher named Phil Todt, who was claimed by both the St. Louis Browns and St. Louis Cardinals.

While the 17-year-old Todt had been discovered and signed by Branch Rickey for the Cardinals, Landis found that Todt had been given an unconditional release when the Cards farmed him out to the Minor leagues. In accordance with a common practice, there was a "gentlemen's agreement" that Todt was still Cardinal property.

Since Todt did not play in the Minors or sign a Minor League contract, however, he was picked up by the Browns—and Landis ruled in their favor. In doing so, he made it clear that he intended to protect players' rights and rid the game of informal agreements among owners.

Landis next cracked down on New York Giants outfielder Benny Kauff, once hailed as the "Ty Cobb" of the Federal League, who was arrested in the offseason and charged with car theft and receiving stolen goods. Even though acquitted, Landis didn't like what he learned of the case from reading the court record and barred Kauff from baseball for life.

At about this time, Landis had a little setback of his own, as there were those who felt that holding onto his post in the District Court while being paid to govern baseball was a conflict of interest. Although he took his time about it, Landis gave up the judgeship early in the year.

Plunging ahead with his new duties, he canceled a deal John McGraw made to obtain hard-hitting Henie Groh from the Cincinnati Reds.

The Giants were struggling to beat off the front-running Pirates as they made a bid for the 1921 championship, and needed greater batting punch. They saw Groh, a Cincinnati holdout, as the answer to their prayers.

Unfortunately, Groh had announced publicly that he wouldn't sign with Cincinnati unless the Reds agreed to trade him.

Landis ruled that it was detrimental to baseball when a player could dictate his transfer to a contender.

McGraw subsequently obtained a quality hitter from Philadelphia, Emil "Irish" Meusel. Even though the last-place Phillies supposedly traded Meusel for his "indifferent" play, Landis took no action, sparking complaints that he used a double standard when making decisions.

While these and several other decisions titillated baseball's rapidly growing legion of fans, it was the 26-year-old, swashbuckling, cocky, fun-loving Babe Ruth and the pennant races that dominated their interest.

In 1921, with the Majors secretly putting a livelier ball into play, Ruth upped his homer production to a mind-boggling 59, five more than his record of the year before and 35 more than his closest American League rival for the homer title, teammate Bob Meusel. (Homer honors in the National League went to the Giants' first baseman, George Kelly, who banged out 23.)

Ruth, who was having one of the best seasons of his career, knocked 170 runs across the plate. His sensational hitting, coupled with 27 wins by Carl Mays, gave the Yankees their first in what would become the longest array of pennants in baseball history.

And when the Giants romped to the flag four lengths ahead of Pittsburgh, New York City had the first of its famous "Subway Series," although all the games would be played in the same ballpark. It was also the first World Series for the new Commissioner, and he quickly established a precedent by taking control of virtually all aspects of the games. He did so without consulting League Presidents John Heydler, or Ban Johnson, the man most responsible for initiating the World Series.

In another "best-of-nine" set, the Giants whipped the Yankees five games to three.

Babe Ruth, a terror to American League pitchers during the regular season, was a big disappointment to Yankee fans during the World Championship games. Forced out of the lineup after the fifth game by an abscess in his left elbow and a knee injury, Ruth had but one homer among his five hits in 16 trips to the plate.

There were two reasons for Ruth's poor showing. First, of course, was the fact that he was unable to play in all the games. But secondly,

The Yankees' Bob Meusel joined Ruth on a barnstorming trip that brought a fine and suspension.

McGraw had Ruth well scouted and knew that Babe murdered the fast ball and could also hit the curve.

Calling every pitch from the bench, McGraw saw to it that the Bambino was fed mostly slow pitches, which upset the Babe's swing-from-the-heels timing.

The Series was hardly over before Landis made a ruling that rocked baseball.

Like his foray against John D. Rockefeller Sr., Landis took after the game's biggest name—Babe Ruth.

Ruth, Bob Meusel and another Yankee player, Bill Piercy, had signed contracts to join several other players and put on exhibition games while they toured various parts of the country. The players were warned they could not make such a tour without authorization, a long-standing rule. Ruth was specifically told that Landis would not approve.

When Ruth heard about Landis' interest in the tour, he made one of his typically irreverent remarks: "What's the old goat got to do with me?"

When Ruth and his teammates went ahead with the tour, the answer to that question wasn't long in coming.

First, Landis held up the money each player was to receive from the proceeds of the World Series, which amounted to more than $3,000.

About a month later, he also fined the trio the amount of their World Series share and suspended them for the first 39 days of the following season, 1922.

With that order, the lesson was clear: No one was bigger than baseball. Not even Babe Ruth.

45 Benched

BY THE MID-20S, only a few years after setting his first home run record, Babe Ruth was the most photographed man in the world. Of all the great athletes who populated America's "Golden Age of Sports," as the 20s were called, Ruth was easily the leader in terms of recognition and popularity.

As sportswriter John Kiernan put it:

> My voice may be loud above the crowd
> And my words just a bit uncouth
> But I'll stand and shout 'til the last man's out
> There never was a man like Ruth.

The reason for such extraordinary acclaim, of course, was Ruth's unique ability to drive baseballs to unprecedented heights and distances; an ability that thrilled the thousands who saw him. Once seen, a Ruthian homer was never forgotten.

Even pop flies, which seemed to go straight up and almost disappear, brought gasps from the fans. And when Ruth swung mightily and missed, his body corkscrewing downward, the crowds would let out a deafening roar, some among them with delight, others with disappointment.

It was not only the way Ruth played baseball that made him better known to most Americans and many Europeans than the President of the United States.

It was simply because he was Ruth—a unique, larger-than-life character who broke all the rules, on the diamond and off; and, with some notable exceptions, got away with it.

From childhood to the threshold of manhood, Ruth was deprived of all the "good things" life had to offer, including food, clothing, shelter, a family and friends. But suddenly, he began to earn more money than he ever dreamed possible; money that came not only from the highest salary in baseball, but from endorsements of products, and fees from public appearances and ghost-written stories. With that money came the ability to buy whatever he wanted, eat and drink what he wanted, go where he wanted to go and entertain his friends any way he saw fit.

Although he never wore underwear after shucking the "union suits" forced on all boys at St. Mary's, he bought expensive silk shirts by the dozen, fancy cars, camel hair coats and caps and ate nothing but what he considered the most expensive food—steaks and chops.

Whether on the road or in New York, Ruth lived and entertained lavishly in the most expensive suites in the most exclusive hotels. He didn't even know many of the so-called friends who surrounded him wherever he went. If he did, he didn't remember their names and resorted to a breezy "Hi ya keed!" to return a greeting. (Ruth had such a weak memory for faces he failed to recognize some of the pitchers who opposed him. He once hit a homer off Washington hurler Horace Lisenbee. After the game, when Lisenbee brought him a ball to sign, Ruth asked, "Where wuz you sittin'?")

Ruth's humorous and irreverent comments to major public figures also endeared him to his admirers.

On posing with President Coolidge one Opening Day, Ruth was moved to comment, "Hot as hell, ain't it Prez?"

And when he met General Ferdinand Foch of France for the first time, he said, "Hey, Gen, I hear you wuz in the war."

Years later, when his salary soared to $80,000 a year, someone pointed out that he made more than President Herbert Hoover. "Why not?" Ruth was said to have commented. "I had a better year."

Another side of Ruth also appealed to the public. He loved kids. When they followed him about, he treated them gently and kindly. And he rarely, if ever, turned down an appeal to visit a seriously sick child in a hospital.

Rules, however, meant nothing to Ruth. He didn't break them deliberately; he just didn't think about them. And when he was chastised about his behavior, he was always contrite and promised to reform. But he never did.

As long as Ruth played well, his manager, Miller Huggins, could do little to slow him down. In early 1925, however, Ruth became ill while traveling north from spring training.

Suffering from what newspapers called "the bellyache heard 'round the world" — that was, in fact, a case of flu and acute indigestion — Ruth was taken from a train, hospitalized and operated on, an event that was said to cost the Yankees $500,000 in ticket sales since Babe missed the opening weeks of the season.

Not everyone was enthralled by Ruth's antics. J. Taylor Spink, editor of *The Sporting News*, baseball's "bible," lashed out at Babe, saying he was setting a bad example for America's youth and "would never be Ty Cobb."

When Ruth returned to the lineup, he was often booed instead of cheered. Undaunted, he continued to indulge his insatiable appetite for women, food and parties. Soon, his performance fell off sharply.

On August 29 in St. Louis, when Ruth stayed out past a curfew set at 1:00 in the morning, Miller Huggins reprimanded the big slugger.

Looking down at his tiny manager, Ruth roared, "You can't make a mug out of me! I never liked you anyhow. For two pins I'd smack you right in the face!"

"I couldn't make a mug out of you if I tried," Miller came back. "God

Owner Jake Ruppert and manager Miller Huggins taught Babe Ruth a lesson.

did that long ago. And if I weighed 40 pounds more, I'd give you a licking right now."

He then told Ruth he was "through" with the Yankees, fined Babe a staggering $5,000 and benched him.

A furious Ruth said owner Jake Ruppert would overrule Huggins and rescind the fine because "they don't fine bootleggers that much."

But Ruppert gave Huggins his full support.

Typically, Ruth apologized to Huggins, agreed to go on a diet and begged to get back into the lineup. But the fine remained and Ruth stayed on the bench until Labor Day. After that, he began to apply himself more seriously to baseball.

When he did, he singlehandedly changed the style of baseball forever.

46 The Cardinals Arrive

A s BABE RUTH and his big bat started to shape a new kind of game on the ballfield, Wesley Branch Rickey set out to change baseball in a way that was entirely different, but equally important.

The year: 1919.

The objective: (a) Locate, sign and develop hundreds of young and talented ballplayers at the lowest possible cost; (b) balance the power among Major League teams; and (c) stabilize the Minor Leagues.

The method: Invest in farm teams at every level and fill the rosters with prospects out of high school, college or a Cardinal tryout camp.

When Rickey broached his innovative idea for what became known as the "farm system," he was 38 years old and manager of the St. Louis Cardinals, a team so poor it held spring training in the gym of a local college.

At the time, Rickey had been in baseball for 16 years, and he had learned a singular truth: Money buys talent. Talent wins pennants. Pennants make money. And money . . .

It was a cycle, Rickey reasoned, that had to be broken if financially weak teams such as the Cardinals ever hoped to compete successfully against clubs like the rich New York Giants and the Yankees.

Rickey was born on December 20, 1881 in Lucasville, Ohio. He went to Ohio Wesleyan on a partial scholarship and supported himself by playing Minor League baseball. While at Wesleyan, he was captain of the baseball team and played football and basketball.

In 1904, after graduation, he caught for Dallas in the Texas League. Called up by the Cincinnati Reds late that summer, he was dropped almost immediately—not because of his ability, but because he told his manager that he wouldn't play ball on Sunday.

Rickey was the son of parents who were strict fundamentalist Methodists and had promised his mother that he would never play ball or attend games on Sunday—a vow he kept throughout his life.

Rickey got back to the "Bigs" in 1905 when his contract was sold to the St. Louis Browns. After a year with Dallas and then with the Browns, Rickey was traded to the New York Highlanders, where he had an exceptionally poor year as a catcher, first baseman and outfielder. In 52 games he batted .182. And behind the plate, with a lame arm that ended his playing career, opposing runners stole 13 bases in one game—still a Major League record.

Each year between baseball seasons, Rickey went back to college to further his education, earning two bachelors degrees and a law degree. During this period, he also coached the Michigan University baseball teams and scouted for Robert Lee Hedges, owner of the St. Louis Browns.

After becoming a front office assistant to Hedges in 1912, Rickey began experimenting with the idea of placing young prospects with Minor League teams, since the rules governing the Majors at the time prevented a club from having more than 35 players under contract (the number changed frequently).

Rickey made "gentleman's agreements" to stock Minor League clubs

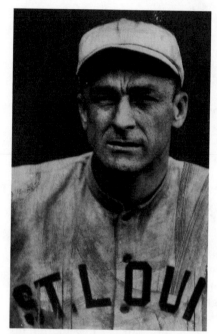

Branch Rickey as he looked when he took over the last-place St. Louis Cardinals in 1919.

Rogers Hornsby led the Cardinals to their first National League pennant.

with players at no expense to the club with the understanding that he could buy each contract back for $1,000 at the end of the season.

When the Browns changed owners in 1916, Rickey joined the Cardinals—and although the Cards were deeply in debt, he managed to get a contract for $15,000 to become the highest-paid executive in baseball. He also bought a $5,000 block of stock at $25 a share. (His parents loaned him the money after mortgaging their farm.)

For St. Louis, Rickey and baseball, it was a fortuitous move.

After finishing third in 1917 under Miller Huggins—his fifth year with the Cardinals—St. Louis dropped to last place and Rickey took over on the diamond.

Rickey now expanded his original plan for farming out players by buying into two Minor League clubs—Houston of the Texas League and Fort Smith of the Western Association.

In 1920, Sam Breadon, who was in the automobile business in St. Louis, bought a controlling interest in the Cardinals. Breadon supported Rickey's approach to the development of talent and almost immediately invested in Syracuse of the International League.

Scores of young players, eager for a chance to play professional

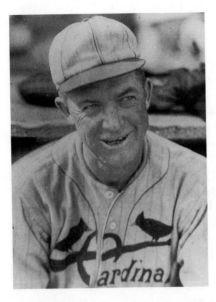

Grover Cleveland Alexander.

baseball, rushed to tryout camps set up by Cardinal scouts. Those who showed promise were signed on the spot. There were no big bonuses or high salaries.

When the young hopefuls arrived at the Cardinal training camps, they were subjected to intensive schooling abetted by several Rickey innovations, including sliding pits, batting cages and chalk talks.

Gradually, the fortunes of the Cardinals began to improve. From seventh place in 1919, the Cards, with Rickey still managing, moved to sixth, then third. They tied for third in 1922, then slipped to fifth, then sixth, and then went back up to fourth.

In 1926, with shortstop Rogers Hornsby piloting the Cardinals and making his debut as a Major League manager, St. Louis won its first National League championship. They then went on to beat the New York Yankees in a dramatic seven-game World Series, a Series in which the Cards' Grover Cleveland Alexander relieved in the seventh inning with the score 3 to 2 Cardinals, the bases loaded and two out.

Alexander struck out Yankee second baseman Tony Lazzeri to end the seventh; set the Yanks down in order in the eighth; but got into trouble in the ninth when he walked Ruth with two out.

Ruth, with slugger Bob Meusel at the plate, took it on himself to attempt a steal. He was thrown out, catcher Bob O'Farrell to shortstop Hornsby, and the game was over.

The Cardinals, thanks to Branch Rickey, had arrived.

47 The Pawns

AT THE CLOSE of the 1926 season, Ty Cobb resigned as player/manager of the Detroit Tigers because he wanted to quit while he was "among the best."

Although he was 40 years old at the time, Cobb could still pound the ball. After his .401 season in 1922, for example, his batting averages each year thereafter were .340, .338, .378 and, in his final year with Detroit, .304.

While it's true that the Tigers finished sixth in 1926, Cobb had Detroit in contention during four of the six years he piloted the club. He was, obviously, still effective as a manager and player and a big drawing card. Why, some wondered, would Cobb leave baseball?

Exactly one month later, another great star quit the game because he "needed a vacation from baseball."

It was Tris Speaker, player/manager of the Cleveland Indians. Like Cobb, Speaker—who was 38—also batted over .300. And until 1926, Speaker was the best manager Cleveland ever had. He won one championship and placed second three times.

With two of the biggest names suddenly out of baseball for vague reasons, the rumor mills began to churn wildly.

Before long, the two players, idolized by thousands, were implicated in a gambling scandal that, in terms of public interest, rivaled the Black Sox affair six years earlier.

St. Louis celebrates after Cards win first World Championship.

Tris Speaker was the player/manager
of the Cleveland Indians.

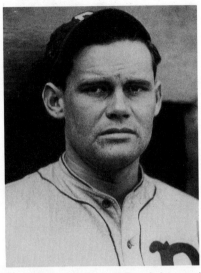

Charges by embittered Dutch Leonard
forced two of baseball's biggest stars
out of baseball.

Two players who were no longer in baseball were also involved. One
of them was Hubert "Dutch" Leonard, a pitcher who last played for the
Tigers in 1925. The other player was Joe Wood, a former pitcher-outfielder
for the Cleveland Indians who ended his career in 1922.

Leonard, angry because Cobb and Speaker—men he considered personal friends—had made no effort to keep him in the Majors toward the
end of his playing days, gave Ban Johnson copies of letters he had
received from Joe Wood and Cobb to back up his statement that a game
played on September 25, 1919, had been fixed and that the four had bet
on Detroit.

Johnson asked Cobb and Speaker to resign and then sent Leonard's
statement and the letters to Judge Landis. He said later that he hoped
the Cobb-Speaker resignations (and their subsequent releases by their
clubs) would end the matter because the two had "done a lot for
baseball."

Still, he subsequently vowed that both men would "never again play
in the American League."

As might be expected, Landis launched an investigation of his own.
At first he decided to withhold what he had learned since all involved in
the incident (which occurred before he took office) were out of baseball.

But the pressure became too great, and although he had not come to

Smoky Joe Wood.

a conclusion about the matter, Landis released the transcript of his inquiry to the press. According to Leonard's statement, the four met beneath the stands in Detroit and it was agreed that he, Leonard, would put up $1,500, while Cobb was to bet $2,000 and Speaker and Wood $1,000 each.

He said once the arrangement was made to place the bets, he left for home since, for him, the season was over.

Later, according to Leonard, he received a letter from Wood that contained a certified check for $1,630, with the explanation that only $600 of Leonard's money had been wagered and that he and Leonard had won $420 between them.

The Wood letter, a copy of which Landis also released, included this line: "Cobb did not get up a cent. He told us that and I believe him."

And here are key paragraphs in the Cobb letter that Leonard sent to Johnson: "Wood and myself are considerably disappointed in our business proposition, as we had $2,000 to put into it and the other side quoted $1,400, and when we finally secured that much money it was about 2 o'clock and they refused to deal with us, as they had men in Chicago to take the matter up with and they had no time, so we completely fell down and of course we felt badly over it . . . ."

Cobb, who was supposedly betting on himself, got only one hit in five trips to the plate in the disputed game, which Detroit won 9 to 5. Speaker, who was supposed to be betting on Detroit, hit two triples and a single.

It's clear, of course, there was no evidence to support Leonard's claim that the game was fixed or that Speaker or Cobb placed any bets.

The reference to "they" and "the other side" in Cobb's letter shows, however, that he probably attempted to place a bet with bookies, a not uncommon practice among ballplayers of that era.

The day the material was released, Cobb told reporters: "I have been in baseball 22 years. I have played the game as hard and square and clean as any man ever did. All I have thought of was to win, every year, every month, every day, every hour. My conscience is clear."

Speaker also denied the charges.

Several months later Landis found Cobb and Speaker innocent of any wrongdoing in the Leonard case. His statement said, in part, that "these players have not been, or are they now, found guilty of fixing a ballgame. By no decent system of justice could such a finding be made . . . ."

Both men were reinstated and were free to negotiate with any club that might want them. In a direct slap at Johnson, Landis made it clear in private conversations with the owners that if the two stars did return to baseball, it could only be in the American League.

The two players, in other words, had become pawns in the bitter power struggle between the Commissioner of Baseball and the President of the American League.

48 A Sad Ending

A LTHOUGH HE PUT UP a gallant battle, Ban Johnson eventually lost his private war with Commissioner Landis.

The first serious defeat occurred in 1924 and stemmed from an incident involving the pennant-bound New York Giants that smacked of another Black Sox scandal.

With two games left against Philadelphia, the Giants were 1½ games ahead of Brooklyn and needed only one victory or one Brooklyn defeat to clinch the flag.

Before the start of the first game, Jimmy O'Connell, a young and promising outfielder/infielder who had appeared in 52 games for the Giants, approached Philadelphia shortstop Heine Sand and said, "It will be worth $500 to you if you don't bear down too hard on us today."

The Giants won the game and the Dodgers lost, which meant the Giants became the first team in modern history to win four pennants in a row.

Young Jimmy O'Connell's offer of   **Cozy Dolan had a bad memory.**
$500 to a Philadelphia player to
"go easy" on the Giants had serious
repercussions.

Before the game, however, Sand reported O'Connell's remark to his manager, Arthur Fletcher; Fletcher later relayed it to League President John Heydler who, in turn, informed Landis.

Landis immediately had an interview with O'Connell, who readily admitted that he did make the $500 offer to Sand, but only because one of the Giants coaches, Cozy Dolan, asked him to.

O'Connell insisted that was all he knew about the matter. Under probing by Landis, however, O'Connell said he thought three of the Giants' top players might know something because they had seen him speak to Sand and wanted to know what Sand had to say.

The three players included right fielder Ross Youngs, second baseman Frankie Frisch and first baseman George Kelly, the very heart of the team.

With the start of the World Series between the Giants and the Washington Senators—winners of their first American League flag—rapidly approaching, Landis quickly widened his inquiry.

After interviewing Cozy Dolan and the three players, Landis reached a decision. Frisch, Youngs and Kelly—who denied any involvement in the matter—were exonerated. O'Connell and Dolan were booted out of baseball—O'Connell for the attempted bribe and Dolan because he

Walter Johnson almost missed his first chance to pitch in a World Series.

repeatedly answered "I can't remember" to all of Landis' pertinent questions.

Ban Johnson learned of the scandal from the newspapers, even though he and John Heydler had been elected as the only members of Landis' Advisory Council. Johnson promptly advised that, in view of the developments, Brooklyn should replace the Giants as the Washington Senators' opponent in the Series.

"And if Brooklyn isn't permitted to play, there should be no Series," he added.

Brushing off Johnson's suggestion (supported by Barney Dreyfuss, owner of the third-place Pittsburgh Pirates), Landis allowed the Series to go on.

For Washington fans and those who admired Walter Johnson, then in his 18th year with the Senators, it was an historic decision. While the great right-hander, then 36 years old, lost the first and third game, he won the seventh and deciding twelve-inning thriller 4 to 3 after relieving in the ninth with the score tied at 3 to 3.

When the Series was over, Ban Johnson did the unthinkable: He asked for a Federal investigation of baseball, the one thing all of those involved in operating the game dreaded most.

Though nothing came from his efforts, Johnson kept the heat on Landis in the months following the World Series by hiring investigators to look into reports that a gambling ring was operating in Los Angeles.

Landis saw Johnson's move as a threat to his power and criticism of his conduct and decided to bring matters to a head at the winter meetings. Either Landis or Johnson was going to run baseball, he thundered.

At first, the American League owners tried to smooth things over between the two combatants. The Yankees' Jake Ruppert said he hoped the two men were "big enough" to bury the hatchet. He went on to point out that Johnson and Landis had no money invested in baseball, but their continuous bickering was hurting the game and endangering those who put their dollars into it.

Later, however, the American League owners censured Johnson publicly for his "misconduct" and removed him from the Advisory Council.

In a lengthy resolution, the owners asked Landis to overlook Johnson's past conduct and accept certain "guarantees" for the future, including the following:

- That his misconduct would cease or his immediate removal from office would follow.
- That legislation would be adopted that would limit his activity to the internal affairs of the American League.

Over the next two years, surprisingly, Johnson was given a $10,000 raise and his contract was extended for another 10 years, to 1935. He was also re-elected to the Advisory Council.

A short time later, Johnson told newsmen Landis had made a "mess" of the Cobb-Speaker matter, adding, "When Landis released that testimony and those letters, I was amazed. The only thing I could see behind that move was a desire for personal publicity."

That outburst brought another showdown and, for the second time, the American League owners sided with Landis.

In July of 1927, Johnson was again in hot water for suspending several players for run-ins with umpires.

Fed up with Johnson's autocracy, which they felt had become irrational, the American League owners decided to ask for his resignation at a meeting on July 8, supposedly called for another purpose.

But Johnson knew what was coming and even though he was only a few rooms away from the meeting room, he refused to join the owners at the appointed hour. He did, however, agree to receive an emissary, Jake Ruppert. When Ruppert arrived in his room, Johnson hastily scribbled his resignation on a letterhead and threw it at the Yankee owner.

The resignation was effective at the end of the 1927 season. Proud and defiant to the end, Johnson declined to be paid the $320,000 due him beyond the end of the season.

While Ban Johnson was many of the things his enemies said he was—

An ill and dispirited Ban Johnson locks
his desk at American League head-
quarters for the last time.

autocratic, harsh, strong-willed, egocentric and biased — he alone, virtually, established the American League.

Most important, for 20 years before Judge Landis arrived on the scene and the seven years after, he fought with all that was in him to drive out of baseball the one element that could destroy it — dishonesty.

In this respect, he was true to the tenets of five of his most important predecessors — Harry Wright, William Hulbert, Al Spalding, John Ward and Abraham Mills.

Johnson's departure from the game, signaled by that short, handwritten note thrown at Jake Ruppert, marked a sad ending to an otherwise illustrious and extraordinarily productive baseball career.

Two years later, suffering from diabetes, Johnson was dead at the age of 67. He was elected to the Hall of Fame in 1937.

49 The Rebel

W HEN JOHN McGRAW LEARNED that Ty Cobb had resigned from the Tigers at the end of the 1926 season, he immediately wanted to sign the aging outfielder.

As a precautionary step, however, he decided to get in touch with Commissioner Landis " . . . even though I could not see how the stories I had heard could seriously involve Cobb."

Ty Cobb (center) said his happiest years in baseball were spent with the
Philadelphia Athletics. Here he poses with (left to right)coach Kid Gleason, second baseman Eddie Collins, pitcher Zack Wheat and Connie Mack, whom, he
said, he "revered."

McGraw said he received this response from Landis. "You asked me a
direct question and I must reply in the same way: Lay off Cobb."

For awhile, Cobb (along with Speaker) considered suing Organized
Baseball, and it appeared as if he would never play again. A month
before spring training in 1927, however, Cobb received a visitor at his
Georgia home. It was Connie Mack, a man he had long admired.

Before Mack left, Cobb had signed to play with the Athletics. The
consensus among newsmen was that the As, needing a gate attraction badly, landed Cobb for $70,000—a great deal more than he had
received at Detroit.

But money was of little interest to Cobb. At this point in his life,
investments in Coca Cola, General Motors and other companies had
made him a rich man. Cobb simply wanted to get back into baseball and
demonstrate once again that he was "the best." (Speaker also returned
to the game, signing with Washington.)

Although he had slowed considerably, Cobb appeared in 133 games and batted .357, the fifth highest average in the League. He also stole 22 bases, only five fewer than League leader George Sisler.

During that long, hot summer, Cobb showed flashes of his old form. On April 4 against the Red Sox in Boston, for example, he drove in four runs with the two singles and a double. In the seventh inning of that game, he stole home and in the ninth made an unassisted double play. (He was to steal home twice more that season.)

Late in the year, he went 17 for 25 in six games. In three of those games, he stole four bases.

As usual, he was also involved in controversy.

Late in April, he had a run-in with an umpire that brought a suspension from Ban Johnson. In a home game against the Red Sox, Cobb had hit a drive over the right field wall in the eighth inning. The umpire yelled "foul!" because the ball curved foul after it left the park, a call that was permissible under an old rule. Had it been allowed, that shot would have tied the score at 3 to 3.

Although Cobb made a mild protest, it was the on-deck batter, Al Simmons, who got the heave-ho for extended and uncomplimentary remarks. (Simmons was also suspended by Johnson.)

Cobb again stepped into the batter's box to hit. Before the pitcher delivered, however, he suddenly jumped back—and, in so doing, brushed against the umpire. Even though Cobb insisted the contact with the ump was accidental, he was ejected.

At the end of the game, which the As lost 3 to 2, disgusted Philadelphia fans bombarded the umpire with debris as he left the field.

Cobb's suspension became known a few days before the Athletics were to play in Detroit, where preparations had been made for a "Ty Cobb Day."

Detroit fans flooded Johnson's office with telegrams which, suprisingly, moved the American League President to lift the suspension the day the Philadelphia-Detroit series opened.

Among the many gifts showered on Cobb that day was a new automobile.

In his first time at bat, Cobb doubled and then scored on a single by Al Simmons. When he took his position in the outfield, the game had to be held up so he could sign scores of scorecards thrust at him by fans in the overflow crowd.

All in all, 1927 was a great year for Ty Cobb; so great, in fact, that he decided to put on his spikes one more time.

By 1928, however, Cobb was 41 with failing legs. Although he appeared in 95 games and hit .323, he knew his career was over. He retired toward the end of the season.

Out of baseball, Cobb moved restlessly about the country, spending

While Ty Cobb refused to have his picture taken with Judge Landis at the Hall of Fame Inauguration, he was pleased to pose with young fans during subsequent visits to Cooperstown. Shortly before his death, Cobb suggested this shot with John J. Rosenburg, the author's son. *Author's collection.*

most of his time hunting, playing golf, and dabbling in various business ventures. Divorced twice and apparently alienated from most of his family, Cobb lived a lonely private life.

He did, however, gain a great deal of satisfaction from the announcement in 1936 that he was among the first five elected to the Hall of Fame. And getting 226 of the possible 230 ballots by the Baseball Writers Association of America satisfied him that he was, at last, considered "the best."

Because he felt Landis took too long to exonerate him in the Dutch Leonard case, Cobb didn't want to be photographed with him and deliberately missed the early ceremonies dedicating the Hall and Museum in 1939.

He was a rebel to the end. And the end came in July 1961 when, at 75, he died of cancer in Cornelia, Georgia.

50 The King

WHEN BABE RUTH REGAINED his health and settled his differences with Miller Huggins, he was 31 years old, an age when the skills of many ballplayers begin to fade.

But Ruth was no ordinary ballplayer. By the end of 1925, for example, he had already hit 300 homers, a mark reached by only 53 other players in the history of the game (as of this writing).

By the time he left baseball 10 years later, at age 40, Ruth would hit 414 more.

Ruth's best drive toward his total of 714 homers occurred between 1926 and 1930; he was between the ages of 31 and 36. In that five-year span, he averaged 51.2 home runs per season, for a total of 256; and 153.6 runs batted in per season, for a total of 768.

It is also significant to note that Ruth walked an average of 125 times a season over that same period.

Although they finished seventh in 1925, the Yankees easily forged to first place the following year, thanks to the purchase of infielders Mark Koenig and Tony Lazzeri, and Ruth's return to form.

Ruth led the League in home runs, runs batted in, total bases and runs scored that year. His batting average of .372 was only 6 percentage points behind Heine Manush, the League leader in that department.

And his play in the World Series against St. Louis—except for the attempted steal of second that brought the seventh game to an abrupt end—was exemplary.

Held to two singles in the first three games, he broke loose with three homers in Game 4 to lead the Yankees to a 10 to 5 victory and even the Series.

In the first inning he walloped the first pitch over the right field bleacher roof with the bases empty. In the third, he boomed another, longer homer, over the bleacher roof in right center, again with no one on. A third homer followed in the sixth with one man on. This one soared high above the center field bleachers and went over the wall, the longest homer seen in that park up to that time.

The third round-tripper also marked the first time anyone had hit three in a World Series.

But Ruth wasn't finished. He rapped out a fourth in Game 7, which the Yankees lost 3 to 2. He also drew his 11th walk, still a Series record.

Despite that glorious performance, it was but a mild prelude to what would burst on the baseball world in 1927. For that year, the Yankees fielded the mightiest team the game has ever seen.

Leading the pack from opening day (when they were greeted by almost 70,000 fans) to the end of the season, the Yankees romped home 19 games ahead of the second-place Philadelphia Athletics with a record of 110 victories and 44 losses.

While the success of the Yankees in 1927 was due to a perfect blend of pitching, batting and fielding, it was the home run production of Ruth and Lou Gehrig that excited the fans and attracted the most attention.

By the second week in August, Gehrig was leading Ruth 38 to 35. It appeared to many that Gehrig, coming into his own at 24 years of age and eight years younger than Ruth, would top the Bambino in the

Lou Gehrig's bat was often as potent as Ruth's.

homer derby by year's end. But Babe Ruth liked nothing better than a challenge—especially when it came from a younger member of his own team.

While Gehrig's home run pace began to drop off toward the end of the season (he finished with 47), Ruth's accelerated.

On September 6, for example, he hit three. On September 7, he hammered out two more for Numbers 48 and 49, enough to put him two ahead of what would prove to be Gehrig's second-place total, and 19 more than the National League's homer leaders, the Cubs' Hack Wilson and the Phillies' Cy Williams, who would tie at 30.

On September 11, he hit Number 50; two days later he collected one in each game of a doubleheader against Cleveland at Yankee Stadium, for 51 and 52.

There were no homers for the next two games. By then, it seemed highly unlikely that he could break his own record of 58 before the season ended. But on September 16, the Yankees' 143rd game, Ruth blasted Number 53 off Ted Blankenship; two days later he rapped another Washington pitcher, Ted Lyons, for Number 54.

When the Detroit Tigers visited New York on September 21, Ruth pounded out two more homers on successive days.

Dramatically enough, the second one—Number 56—came in the bottom of the ninth inning with one on to give the Yankees an 8–7 victory. Anticipating that the crowd would come pouring onto the field, Ruth kept his bat with him as he rounded the bases. As Ruth approached third, a small boy in knickers who was sitting near the Yankee dugout (and who had pleaded with Ruth to "do something" in three previous hitless trips to the plate), jumped the railing and ran to the slugger. After pounding Ruth joyfully on the back, the youngster grabbed the bat and hung on.

To the roaring delight of the crowd, Ruth, without breaking stride, carried the boy and bat around third, across the plate and into the dugout where both disappeared.

During the next three games, Ruth went dry.

Now, with only three games left, Ruth needed two homers to tie his own record and three to break it.

The As' Lefty Grove, one of the toughest pitchers in the League, was scheduled to face the Yankees in the first of the three remaining games. He turned out to be just another hurler as Ruth drove one of his pitches over the wall for Number 57.

With two games left, Ruth needed one homer to tie his own record and one to break it. Could he do it?

The answer came on September 29 when the Senators opened a two-game series in New York. With right-hander Horace Lisenbee on the mound for Washington in the first game, Ruth boomed Number 58 over the fence. In the same game, he collected the tiebreaker off another right-hander, Paul Hopkins.

But the season had one more day and one more game to go—September 30 and Game 154.

On that historic occasion, Babe Ruth lashed a pitch into the right field seats near the foul line as Washington southpaw Tom Zachary yelled, "Foul! Foul!"

But Number 60 was not foul. And when Ruth touched home to a thunderous ovation, he had established a record no one has equaled.

Some, of course, will point to the fact that Roger Maris notched 61 homers in 1961 while playing for the Yankees.

That was a great accomplishment, no doubt about it. But, the records show that Maris, playing a 162-game schedule, appeared in 10 more games and went to bat 50 more times than Ruth. And, with the exception of the one homer, Ruth topped Maris' 1961 record in several other important respects, including home run percentage, 11.1 to 10.3.

Without a doubt, Babe Ruth to this day remains the single-season home run king.

51 The Epic Feat

BABE RUTH HAD A CREDITABLE World Series in 1927, when he collected six hits, which included two home runs, and batted .400 as the Yankees rolled over the Pirates four straight.

Still, he didn't come close to the show he put on a year later. In fact, no one has matched the Babe's World Series performance of 1928, when the Yankees faced the Cardinals, National League Champions for the second time in three years.

With Ruth knocking out 54 home runs (it was the fourth time he went over the 50 mark) and Lou Gehrig batting .374 while driving in 142 runs, the Yankees fought off a late-season drive by the improving Athletics to capture the American League flag by 2½ games.

In the World Series, the potent bats of Ruth and Gehrig continued their thunder as the Yankees again won the Championship by taking four games in a row by scores of 4–1, 9–3, 7–3 and 7–3.

Gehrig had six hits, including four homers (matching Ruth's record set in 1926 in six games), batted .545 and drove in nine of the Yankee runs.

Babe, on the other hand, collected 10 hits in 16 trips to the plate and scored nine runs, the most in any four-game Series (tied by Gehrig in 1932).

Reggie Jackson hit three homers in a World Series, the only player to match Ruth's record. Ruth, however, did it twice.

Three of Ruth's hits were doubles and three—all coming in Game 4—were home runs.

While it would be 49 years before another player would hit three homers in a single Series game (Reggie Jackson, playing for the New York Yankees against the Los Angeles Dodgers in 1977), Ruth had now done it twice.

What's more, he also compiled a .625 batting average during the 1928 Series, another record that still stands.

Some believe Babe reached his peak during 1928. Perhaps. And while it's true that he never again appeared in every game during a season, the fact remains that he continued to lead the League in home runs and slugging average for the next three seasons. Over the next five, his batting average remained well above the .300 level.

If Ruth's career was on the down-slope after 1928, opposing pitchers didn't acknowledge it. For in four of the next five years, he was the most frequently walked man in the Majors, as this table will show.

Year	Bases on Balls National League High	Ruth
1929	113	72
1930	105	136
1931	80	128
1932	100	132
1933	75	114

After Connie Mack's Athletics won the American League flag in 1929, 1930 and 1931, the Yankees were back—this time, with another powerhouse team under manager Joe McCarthy, who had piloted the Chicago Cubs to a championship in 1929, but got fired after a second-place finish the next year.

As fate would have it, the Cubs were to be the Yankee opponents in 1932 after a bizarre season in which manager Rogers Hornsby, with the team in first place, was given the gate to be replaced by Charlie Grimm.

Late in August, the Cubs picked up a former Yankee, Mark Koenig, to bolster the shortstop position. But despite the fact that Koenig did a superb job and batted .353, the Cubs voted him only half a share of the World Series money. This brought some well-publicized remarks from Ruth, the most pointed being that the Cubs were "cheapskates."

After the Yankees won the first two games in New York by scores of 12 to 6 and 5 to 2, the Series shifted to Chicago. By then, both teams were riding each other unmercifully. The Chicago fans also began to heap abuse on the Yankees, and when Ruth came to bat in the first inning to face Charley Root with two men on, they threw lemons at the round-faced slugger.

Charley Root was on the mound for Chicago when Ruth supposedly "called" his shot in the 1932 World Series.

According to the *New York Herald Tribune*, Ruth "paused to jest with the raging Cubs, pointed a finger to the right field bleachers and grinned."

With the count 2 and 0, Ruth blasted the ball out of the park to give the Yankees a 3 to 0 lead.

In the fifth inning, with the score tied at 4 to 4 and one out, Ruth again stepped into the maelstrom of malice. As he did so, a single lemon, glinting in the sunlight, bounded toward him.

" . . . in no mistaken motion," the *New York Times* later reported, "the Babe notified the crowd that the nature of his retaliation would be a wallop right out of the confines of the park."

Charley Root whipped the first pitch past Ruth's knees for a called strike, bringing a shriek of glee from the Chicago rooters.

Unperturbed, Ruth raised one finger and bobbed his head toward the Cub dugout and stands. At each successive pitch, he raised the appropriate number of fingers and continued the pantomime.

When Root made his fifth pitch, Ruth swung.

"Then the mightiest blow of all fell," the *Times* reporter wrote. "It was a tremendous smash that bore straight over the center in an enormous arc, came down alongside the flagpole and disappeared.

"The crowd, unmindful of anything except that it had just witnessed an epic feat, let loose with a great salvo of applause."

Many claimed that when Ruth waved his hands that day, he had "called his shot."

Pitcher Root said, no, Ruth was merely indicating the count as it progressed.

And while only Ruth really knew, the "epic feat" was the most discussed incident in the 22-year career of baseball's most memorable figure.

52 The Legacy

WHEN JOHN McGRAW ARRIVED at the Polo Grounds on July 19 1902, he saw a small, wooden grandstand behind home plate, and wooden "bleaching boards" around the rest of the field.

On the average, the Giants drew 2,000 to 3,000 die-hard, but disillusioned fans.

By 1922, 25 years later, a horseshoe of concrete and steel that could seat 50,000 had replaced the old, wooden structures, and it was fairly common for those seats to be filled with enthusiastic Giants fans.

How did it happen?

McGraw often said his method of managing fell into three parts:

- Building teams.
- Handling personnel.
- Winning games.

Of the three, he said, winning games was easiest.

McGraw had a method, a style of play, and his players had to conform. If they didn't they were gone. When players ignored or missed McGraw's signs, they could expect a tongue-lashing and a fine. A well-known case was that of Sammy Strang. Ordered to bunt, Strang hit away and drove the ball over the fence for a home run that won the game. Despite his excuses, Strang was fined $25 for not following orders.

From the time he was a schoolboy pitcher in Truxton, New York, to the day he left baseball, McGraw experimented with new techniques and plays that would give his team an edge.

With Sammy Strang, who played for the Giants early in 1900, for example, he introduced the delayed steal from first base.

Still at it 22 years later, McGraw developed a new cutoff play using shortstop Dave Bancroft. Until then, with second base occupied, the pitcher was the cutoff man on throws to the plate when a batter singled.

Frankie Frisch was a McGraw favorite, but the feeling wasn't always mutual.

Like Frank Frisch, Bill Terry refused to speak to McGraw for months.

(McGraw claimed the play stifled two Yankee rallies during the 1922 Series.)

McGraw's relationship with his players was generally good, though he liked some more than others. Christy Mathewson and Casey Stengel were two disparate examples with whom he got along famously on both a personal and professional level.

While McGraw was fond of Frankie Frisch and had a high regard for Bill Terry, there were long periods when both men refused to speak to him because of a salary dispute or a disagreement sparked by his autocratic ways.

Frisch, for example, didn't say a word to McGraw during much of 1926. The following year, after he was traded with pitcher Jimmy Ring to St. Louis for Rogers Hornsby, Frisch met Mrs. McGraw by chance in a restaurant. She insisted he call on his old boss after a ballgame.

"When I left the club that night, I felt like a doomed man," Frisch recalled. But when he got to the McGraws and rang the doorbell, he was greeted by a shirt-sleeved McGraw.

"His arms were outstretched, he grabbed my hands and pulled me into the house," Frisch said.

The next two hours, according to Frisch, were "the most enjoyable I ever spent in my life," and not once did he and McGraw talk about baseball.

Casey Stengel, one of a long line of managers tutored by McGraw, welcomes an Opening Day crowd at the New York Mets' Shea Stadium.

As to Terry, he and McGraw stopped speaking some time early in 1931. On June 1 the following year, the Giants were in last place and had just lost a game to Philadelphia when McGraw called Terry into his office.

Terry, braced for the worst, was astonished to hear McGraw say, "I'm retiring from the job. If you want it, you can have it."

Terry recovered enough to say he would take it. Later, he was to say of that dramatic moment: "I never felt smaller and he showed me in 10 seconds what a big and genuine man he was."

Except for managing the National League in the first All-Star game against Connie Mack and the American League, McGraw never again appeared on the diamond. He died of cancer of the prostate and uremic poisoning on February 25, 1954. He was 61.

Veteran sportswriters Allison Danzig and Joe Reichler said of McGraw in their book, *The History of Baseball,* that he was to baseball "what the Wright Brothers were to the airplane industry."

"He was a pioneer, an innovator, an exciting, creative ballplayer and manager," they added. "He gave the game the hit-and-run play that revolutionized baseball."

McGraw won more National League pennants (10) than any other manager in history. Above and beyond that, he gave the game an extraordinarily long list of successful managers; managers he had tutored and encouraged and even, through his enormous influence, placed in jobs after they left the Giants.

The best known among the early ones were Roger Bresnahan, Kid Gleason and Christy Mathewson. Later, the list included Dave Bancroft,

John Lobert, Billy Southworth, Bill McKechnie, Fred Fitzsimmons, Frankie Frisch, Mel Ott and, of course, Bill Terry.

In 1943, only two of the eight clubs in the National League had a manager at the helm who had not been a member of the Giants under McGraw.

Six years later, McGraw's most illustrious "graduate," Casey Stengel, took over the New York Yankees and matched his mentor's record of 10 League Championships.

Thus, like the innovations he brought to baseball, the managers who followed in his footsteps were an important part of his legacy.

53 Mr. Baseball

THERE CAN BE NO DISPUTING the fact that Commissioner Ken Landis exercised excellent judgment and displayed a great deal of courage on numerous occasions in the conduct of his office. By the same token, however, the Commissioner had a few blind spots that led to foolish mistakes, contradictory rulings and controversy.

A case in point was his protracted and often bitter battle with Branch Rickey over Rickey's farm system.

Starting in 1926, the St. Louis Cards won five National League Championships and three World Series in eight years.

Rickey's system was so successful that the Cards did not find it necessary to buy a player outright between 1919 and 1942. Other teams, notably the Yankees, Dodgers, Tigers and Browns, soon followed Rickey's example.

It was Landis' contention, however, that the system contrived by Rickey had the potential of being abused. He worried that talented Major League prospects would be buried in the Minors for years, and that competition among teams in the same league might be distorted.

In the spring of 1938, Landis found fault with Rickey's arrangements with eight farm clubs and made 90 players free agents. (Two of these players later starred in the Majors; Pete Reiser with the Brooklyn Dodgers and Skeeter Webb with Detroit.)

Cardinal owner Sam Breadon angrily protested the decision and criticized Landis for ignoring the Minors. He pointed out that despite the boom years preceding 1930, the Minors had dropped from a high of 50 Leagues to an all-time low of seven or eight. He said the farm system

Members of the World Champion 1934 Cardinals included (left to right) **Dizzy Dean, Leo Durocher, Ernie Orsatti, Bill Delancey, Ripper Collins, Joe Medwick, Manager Frank Frisch, Jack Rothrock and Pepper Martin. All but Durocher and Rothrock were products of the Rickey farm system.**

was the "salvation" of the Minor Leagues and gave all the credit to Rickey.

Saying that some 40 Minor Leagues were ready to start the 1938 season, Breadon added, "Branch Rickey should receive a vote of thanks from the Commissioner's office for what he has done for baseball, and not censure."

Despite this criticism, Landis continued to snipe at the Cardinals and other clubs. Four years later, in fact, he made free agents of 91 Tiger farm hands.

Undaunted by Landis, Rickey continued to develop his system and at one point had links with 33 teams and 600 to 700 players.

Whether right or wrong, Rickey demonstrated that his idea worked and was, indeed, the "salvation" of the Minors, as Breadon had said.

In addition, it accomplished two other Rickey objectives:

- It helped the Cardinals.
- It helped baseball by tipping the balance of power away from the teams with the biggest bank accounts.

Landis' rulings on the disputed ownership of players — contradictory at times — also aroused controversy and criticism. In 1936, for instance,

Cleveland Indians pitcher Bob Feller with his parents.

he decided that Bob Feller belonged to the Cleveland Indians after a complaint was lodged by the Des Moines club of the Western League.

The Des Moines protest was filed after Feller, then only 17 years old, struck out eight of nine Cardinals when he pitched against them for Cleveland in three innings of an exhibition game.

Des Moines said it had tried to sign Feller a year earlier but had been thwarted in doing so when Cleveland grabbed him in violation of a rule that prohibited the Minors from signing sandlot players.

Feller, in fact, had signed with Fargo-Moorhead in the Northern League while he was still in high school and only 16. The contract was transferred to New Orleans, a Cleveland affiliate.

After the exhibition game, the contract was again transferred, this time to Cleveland for $1,500.

It was clear from the Landis investigation that while Cleveland did not violate the rules technically, it had maneuvered the Feller contract through the Minors by "recommending" each move.

Since both Feller and his father "zealously," as Landis put it, wanted the Cleveland contract upheld, the Judge ruled in favor of the Indians.

In a somewhat similar case involving Cleveland, the Judge made another player—Tommy Henrich—a free agent.

After hitting sensationally for three clubs affiliated with Cleveland, Henrich believed he was being kept from an opportunity to play in the Majors and asked Landis to investigate.

Landis found that the Indians had "covered up" the hard-hitting outfielder, but since he was not under direct contract he was free to sign with anyone—anyone, that is, but the Indians. Henrich signed with the Yankees for a bonus of $25,000 and became one of the team's greatest stars.

To anyone who knew him, it was obvious that Landis was exceptionally vain about his position in baseball. In 1942, he refused to give *The Sporting News* permission to publish the *Official Baseball Guide* because the *News* printed a review of a story in the *Saturday Evening Post* that referred to Editor J. Taylor Spink as "Mr. Baseball."

Piqued by this affront to his station in the game, Landis had his office publish the *Guide,* which came out far too late to be of value to sportswriters, the principal users.

This effort, which lasted only a few years, brought a blast from Red Smith of the *Philadelphia Record,* who wrote, "Judge Kenesaw Mountain Landis is a fool. And if that be treason, let him go ahead and fine me $29,000,000."

In reality, Landis was not a fool. And despite his many idiosyncrasies and faults, the white-maned jurist made an enormously beneficial contribution to baseball during his 25-year reign, which ended when he died at age 78 on November 25, 1944.

Kenesaw Mountain Landis saw himself as "Mr. Baseball," and so did thousands of fans, most of them convinced he loved the game as much as they did.

54 The Ultimate Weapon

TWO YEARS AFTER Babe Ruth hit his 60 home runs, things began to go wrong for the big outfielder and the Yankees.

To begin with, injuries and illness kept Ruth sidelined for much of the early part of the season. In addition, the Yankees of 1929 were not the Yankees of 1927, and the team slipped badly in the standings.

Then, in September, Miller Huggins died. Art Fletcher, one of the coaches, took his place for the last 11 games. When the season ended, the Yankees were in second place, 18 games behind the Athletics.

Ruth, then 34, led both Leagues in homers with 42, drove in 154 runs, and compiled a .345 average in 135 games. Even though his home run total was down by eight from the year before, these were very impressive statistics.

Babe signs one of his many contracts as Ed Barrow and Jake Ruppert look on.

Ruth, however, had another goal, and he was outspoken about it; he wanted to become playing manager of the Yankees.

Jake Ruppert said no, he wasn't in favor of playing managers. As a result, when Art Fletcher announced he didn't want the job in 1930, the Yankees appointed Bob Shawkey, who had managed in the Minors.

Although disappointed, Ruth didn't make much of a fuss, but the following spring he said he wouldn't sign a contract unless the Yankees paid him $100,000.

At the time, the salaries of his teammates ranged from a low of about $10,000 to a high of about $20,000.

After brief negotiations, conducted directly with Jake Ruppert, Ruth won agreement on an $80,000 two-year pact. He also got Ruppert to restore the $5,000 Huggins had fined him in 1925.

The agreement on Ruth's salary caused a sensation. All sorts of comparisons were made, the most publicized being with President Herbert Hoover's pay of $75,000. But Ruth earned his salary that year as he continued to belt home runs and attract big crowds wherever he went. And while the team slipped to third under Shawkey, Ruth again was the top

**Ruth ended his Major League playing
days back in Boston, but with the Braves
of the National League.**

home run hitter in the League with 49. He also raised his batting
average to .359, the third highest in the League.

At the end of the season, the Yankees fired Shawkey. Ruth was certain he would get the manager's job, but Ruppert and Barrow still had
not changed their minds about Babe and turned instead to Joe McCarthy, let go in midseason by the Chicago Cubs in favor of Hornsby.

Ruth was crushed. Not only did the Yankees again refuse to consider
him, they got a replacement from the National League!

For the next three years, Ruth continued his campaign to take over
the Yankees on the field.

At the same time, the Yankees, blaming it on the depression, began to
cut his salary—from $75,000 in 1932, to $50,000 in 1933, to $35,000 in
1934.

During this period Ruth became less and less effective at bat. Still,
there were times when he would rise to the occasion and thrill the
crowd with another of those tremendous home runs. In the first All-Star
game in 1933, for example, he hit a two-run round-tripper off Bill
Hallahan in the third inning to pace the American League to a 4 to 3
victory.

By the end of 1934, however, he seemed to be washed up. His batting
average had fallen to .288 and his home run production had dropped to
22. His skills as a fielder and baserunner had also diminished
considerably.

In the belief that Ruppert and Barrow would call on him to replace
McCarthy, he turned down an offer to manage the Yankees' Newark

team in the International League and let slip opportunities to pilot the Red Sox, Tigers and possibly the Athletics.

When Joe McCarthy was signed to a three-year contract in 1935, Ruth's dream ended. In February, after Ruppert gave him an unconditional release, he signed with the Boston Braves as "Assistant Manager" and Vice President with the understanding that he could also play—an implication that he would finally have an opportunity to manage, possibly the following year.

On Opening Day in Boston, with a large crowd on hand, Babe reached back for that something extra and singled, then hammered out a two-run homer to give the Braves a 4 to 2 victory over the Giants, with none other than the great Carl Hubbell on the mound. Boston fans went wild.

From then on, however, it was all downhill. Ruth was through and he knew it.

In the final game of a series with the Pirates in Pittsburgh, Ruth faced Guy Bush, a former Chicago pitcher who had bruised Ruth's arm badly with a fast ball during the 1932 World Series.

In four times at bat, the 40-year-old Ruth rapped Bush for a single and three homers. The third homer cleared the roof of the double-decked portion of the stadium in right field, crossed a street, and bounced off the roof of a house. It was the longest homer ever seen at Forbes Field. That mighty blast, said to have been measured at 600 feet, was home run number 714, Ruth's last in his 22 seasons.

Without doubt, Babe Ruth was the biggest attraction baseball has ever known. Records aside, no one ever hit a baseball with such force and consistency in so many dramatic situations.

More important, Ruth—who died of cancer in 1947—changed the game as no other player had before him. And he did it with the ultimate offensive weapon, a weapon baseball thought little about before 1919: the home run.

55 The Color Line

AT ABOUT THE TIME many people are thinking about retirement, Branch Rickey left the St. Louis Cardinals and joined the Brooklyn Dodgers as President and General Manager. Then 61, Rickey parted company with the Cards when Sam Breadon failed to renew his contract after the 1942 season.

In the 25 years Rickey spent with the Cards, the Red Birds finished in the first division in all but seven seasons. And, starting with 1926, the teams spawned by Rickey's revolutionary farm system brought St. Louis six League championships.

The last of these, in 1942, was a young team that nosed out the Brooklyn Dodgers, Champions the year before, by two games. And they did it by winning 43 of their final 51.

When the Cards, managed by Billy Southworth, met the Yankees in the World Series, they were the underdogs and with good reason: the Bronx Bombers had won 32 of their previous 36 World Series games.

But the mighty Yankees were in for a rude awakening. After dropping the opener to right-hander Red Ruffing 7 to 4, the Cards swept the next four by scores of 4–3, 2–0, 9–6 and 4–2.

The Rickey-built 1942 championship team was also the nucleus of teams that won two more pennants and another World Series during the next two years.

Frank Navin, owner of the Tigers, had once described Rickey as "the smartest man in baseball."

While Navin might have been right, he could have added that Rickey was also a hard, dedicated worker with an unusually clear vision of the future and the world in which he lived.

When Rickey went to the Dodgers, for example, the manpower demands of World War II had begun to drain scores of Major and Minor League players away from their teams. Rickey's response was to continue the policy he originated with the Cardinals—bolster the Dodgers farm system.

Early in 1945, less than three years after he joined the Dodgers, Rickey's fertile mind turned in a somewhat different but related direction. Lunching with broadcaster Walter "Red" Barber in downtown Brooklyn, Rickey confided, "I'm going to tell you something only the Board of Directors of the Brooklyn ballclub and my family know: I'm going to bring a Negro to the Brooklyn Dodgers. I don't know who he is, or where he is. But, he's coming."

Rickey may or may not have known it, but others had tried and failed to bring Negroes into Organized Baseball.

The first to break into the Majors was Moses Fleetwood Walker, a catcher for Toledo of the American Association in 1884. "Fleet" played in 42 games for Milwaukee and batted .263.

A young brother, Welday Wilberforce Walker, joined the club later the same year as an outfielder. Welday played in only five games and batted .222.

The Major League career of the Walker brothers came to an end late in the season when supporters of the Richmond team sent the Milwaukee manager a letter threatening violence if they appeared on the diamond. The letter, signed by four Richmond fans, said in part, "We hope you will listen to our words of warning so there will be no trouble. We only write this to prevent much bloodshed, as you alone can prevent."

Needless to say, the Walkers didn't play in Richmond, and when the season ended, they were let go.

But several black men were scattered among Minor League teams during this period and Fleet Walker was one of them, catching at Newark for a talented pitcher named George Stovey, who was also black.

Cap Anson of the Chicago White Stockings was instrumental in establishing the so-called "color line" against non-Caucasions. When John Montgomery Ward tried to sign Stovey for the Giants, Anson learned of the proposed deal and used his considerable influence to block it. And when Anson took the White Stockings to Newark for an exhibition game, he threatened to call off the game if Stovey and Walker were in the lineup.

Anson's widely publicized attitude slowly but surely drove black players out of Organized Baseball. By 1891, there was not one Negro playing professionally with white teams, according to Lee Allen, the former historian of the National Baseball Museum.

In recalling Rickey's revelation of his plan to bring blacks back into baseball, Barber, the "ole redhead," said, "It was a revolution and Branch Rickey planned it like a revolution."

Barber was right.

56 The Revolution Begins

A LWAYS AN ELOQUENT and forceful speaker, Branch Rickey had little difficulty in selling his ideas to the Board of Directors of the Brooklyn ballclub after he became President of the organization. And he heard no objection when he made the offhand remark that his scouts might turn up "a Negro player or two" as they "beat the bushes."

Rickey knew, of course, that there were more than 20 clubs operating in four black leagues. This meant that almost 500 blacks were playing baseball professionally.

As he had implied to Red Barber, however, Rickey kept his cards close to his chest while he laid out his plans.

He began by sending out more than 20,000 letters to schools and youth organizations asking that they recommend promising players.

Rickey then announced that he was organizing the United States League, an all-Negro circuit, and entering a team called the "Brown Dodgers." This ploy allowed his scouts to search out high-quality black ballplayers without raising any suspicions about his main objective, which was to put a black player in the Majors and open up a huge pool of new talent.

With considerable foresight, gained from his great depth of experience in baseball, Rickey understood, perhaps better than anyone, that the first black player introduced to the Majors after so many years of prejudice would have to be someone unique.

What he was looking for, the world was soon to learn, was a player whose makeup combined several basic qualities, including:

- Exceptional baseball skills.
- A high degree of intelligence, motivation and determination.
- The ability and willingness to discipline himself in a hostile environment.
- Courage.

Obviously, that was a tough bill for anyone to fill—black or white.

One of the many names that came to Rickey's attention was that of Jack Roosevelt Robinson, a shortstop with the Kansas City Monarchs, an all-Negro team. Robinson was 26 years old, and had been the only four-letter man at UCLA. In track, he had broken the Pacific Coast Conference broad-jump record; in basketball, he had been the top scorer in the league.

During one football season, while playing in the backfield for UCLA, Robinson averaged 12 yards a carry to lead the nation's college players in rushing.

Baseball, however, appeared to be his best sport; he was touted as being a steady hitter, aggressive and fast on the bases, and he possessed a better than average arm.

When Robinson was no longer eligible to play college ball (he had played four years and that was the limit), he left school over his mother's protests. She had wanted him to become a lawyer or doctor. Robinson did not think of himself as a long-term student, however, and took a job as an athletic director in the National Youth Administration, a program set up by the Federal Government.

Later, in 1941, he played football with the Los Angeles Bulldogs, a professional team. But the attack on Pearl Harbor took place right after the football season and, before long, Jack was in the U.S. Army.

**Jackie Robinson as he looked while play-
ing with the Kansas City Monarchs.**

After basic training, Robinson became enrolled in the Officers Candidate School at Fort Riley, Kansas. Bone chips in his ankle kept him
from serving overseas. In 1944, he was discharged as a First Lieutenant.

After a short stint as a basketball coach at a black college in Texas,
Robinson joined the Monarchs.

In the years since the initial report on Robinson, America has learned
a lot more about him. It was discovered, for example, that he was born
in Cairo, Georgia, on January 31, 1919, the youngest of five children. Not
long after his birth, his father deserted the family and his mother moved
it to Pasadena, California, where she took a job as a domestic. While she
was at work, Jack was left in the care of his sister, Willie Mae, who was
two years older.

How much Rickey knew of all this is open to conjecture. But he must
have known a great deal, for during the summer of 1945, Rickey issued
an invitation to Robinson to meet him in the Dodger offices in Brooklyn.

Robinson, thinking it might mean a chance to play with the Brown
Dodgers and prove a step up from the Monarchs, accepted.

The now historic meeting between Rickey, then 61, and Robinson,
who was 26, took place on August 24 and lasted for three hours. When it
was concluded, the most significant revolution in baseball history was
underway.

57 Two Cheeks

I T IS SAFE TO SAY that there never was — or will be — another interview between a prospective employer and employee like the one that took place between Jackie Robinson and Branch Rickey that summer day in 1945.

Rickey was obviously impressed by Robinson, who was a half inch short of being 6 feet tall, weighed close to 200 pounds and seemed to be all wire and muscle.

Rickey also reacted favorably to the intelligent way Robinson responded to the intensive, unorthodox grilling he gave the young ballplayer.

The questions, as reported by Rickey biographer Arthur Mann, who was then Rickey's Executive Assistant, appeared to confirm a decision already made.

Early on, for example, Rickey asked, "Jackie, do you have a girl?"

"I don't know," the startled Robinson answered.

"What do you mean, you don't know?" Rickey barked from behind his desk.

Robinson explained that he had been courting Rachel Isum, a girl he met on the campus at UCLA, for about four years, but wasn't sure where the relationship was going.

Rickey promptly suggested that Jackie should marry Rachel "as quick as you can."

Rickey (long a happily married man) believed all ballplayers should be married, especially a black player who might make the grade with the Dodgers. If that were to happen, Rickey knew Robinson would need all the support he could get, especially from a loving wife.

Rickey then told Jackie he would like to sign him to play for the Dodgers' Montreal team in the Triple A International League. If he did well he would then be considered for a job with the parent club.

Realizing that even Montreal was quite a jump from the Kansas City Monarchs and the Brown Dodgers, Robinson was quick to say he'd like to accept the opportunity.

But Branch Rickey was a careful man, and while he liked to tackle new ventures, he didn't like to fail. After he outlined what he had in mind for the former UCLA star, he told Jackie that the two of them must have a firm understanding — an agreement — on just how they would proceed if Jack was to prove successful in breaking baseball's "color line."

Calling on his legal training, Rickey then threw a series of "what if?" questions at Robinson. Questions such as:

What if a hotel refused him a room?

What if a waiter refused to serve him with the white ballplayers?
What if a bus driver ordered him to take a back seat in his bus?

According to Mann, Rickey then shifted gears and opened another, more pointed, line of questioning.

"Suppose they throw at your head?"

"Mr. Rickey, they've been throwing at my head for a long time," Robinson replied.

"Suppose I'm an opposing player in the heat of an important ballgame," Rickey hammered on. "Suppose I collide with you at second base. When I get up, I yell, 'You dirty black bastard.' What do you do then?"

Puzzled for a moment, Robinson asked, "Mr. Rickey, do you want a ballplayer who's afraid to fight back?"

It was then that Rickey capsuled the point of view that would prove to be the key to Robinson's—and his—success.

"I want a ballplayer with guts enough NOT to fight back," he roared. "You've got to do this job with base hits and stolen bases and fielding ground balls, Jackie. Nothing else!"

Rickey then came around his desk, according to Mann, whipped off his jacket and confronted Robinson, who remained seated.

"Now I'm playing against you in the World Series," he growled. "I'm a hotheaded player. I want to win the game, so I go into you, spikes first. But you don't give ground. You stand there and jab the ball into my ribs and the umpire yells, 'Out!' I flare—all I see is your face, that black face, right on top of me—so I haul off and punch you right in the cheek."

Rickey threw a fist to Jackie's face for emphasis.

"What do you do?" Rickey roared.

Robinson hesitated, then said, "Mr. Rickey, I've got two cheeks—is that it?"

Yes, Rickey said, that was it.

On October 23, at a press conference in Montreal, Hector Racine, President of the Royals, announced that Jackie Robinson had been signed to play for the club.

Jackie was given a $3,500 bonus and a contract for $600 a month and would report to Montreal at the start of spring training in Florida, Racine said.

Early in 1946, Robinson took Rickey's advice and married Rachel. Two weeks later, they were on their way to join the Royals.

When Jackie and his new wife made that first trip to spring training, there was ample evidence of what he would have to endure.

"We had little time for adjustment in the private area of our lives, as we were plunged into the extremely uncertain, and frequently hostile, public environment predicted by Branch Rickey," Rachel said in a newspaper article years later.

They were bumped from an airplane in Pensacola, Florida, and had to board a bus to their destination. Although the bus was empty, they were asked to move to the back, which they did "without outward protest."

"Upon our arrival in Daytona Beach, battered as we were, we laughed over our small and largely symbolic triumphs behind the closed door of our first tiny room in a private home of a black family, isolated from the team's hotel," Mrs. Robinson said.

As the team began to move around Florida for exhibition games, several were canceled and there were more problems.

"We were locked out of the ballpark in Jacksonville, Florida and run out of Sanford, Florida," Mrs. Robinson said.

By the time they left the South for Montreal, they were "bruised, stimulated, and more contemplative than when we arrived."

More important, perhaps, Robinson demonstrated that spring that he could live up to his pledge to Branch Rickey. He had shown "two cheeks."

It was only the beginning.

58 The Barrier Is Broken

I F THERE WERE ANY DOUBT that Jackie Robinson could play baseball well enough to stay in the International League, one step down from the Majors, it was dispelled in his first game against Jersey City.

For even though he made an error, Robinson got four hits, including a two-run homer, and stole two bases as Montreal breezed to a 14 to 1 victory. And twice, while on first base, he caused pitchers to balk while leading away from the bag.

Robinson's method of taunting pitchers as he threatened to steal was unique. With arms extended to either side, he jumped up and down erratically in a way that seemed to say "I'm going! I'm going! I'm going!"

His feet, although encased in size 13 shoes, were as quick as a tap dancer's, and he was rarely picked off. Tantalizing and unnerving to pitchers, his lead-off movements delighted fans and were—like Babe Ruth's home runs—forever remembered once seen.

The pace Robinson set in that opening game never slackened. When the season was over, he had won the League's batting title with a .349

average and was tops among second basemen, fielding .985. Now the question became: Was he good enough to break into the Brooklyn Dodger lineup?

The answer from Montreal manager Clay Hopper and all who watched him was a resounding "yes." Unfortunately, a formidable obstacle cropped up toward the end of the year.

A committee established by the Majors issued a "state-of-the-game" report to club owners, pointing up what were perceived to be problem areas. One of the areas addressed concerned the entry of blacks into the Major Leagues.

"Certain groups in this country, including political and social-minded drumbeaters, are conducting pressure campaigns in an attempt to force Major League clubs to sign Negro players," the committee said in its report.

If the club owners gave in to this pressure, the committee implied, it would be bad for both the Majors and the black leagues then in existence.

The committee then struck its most telling blow with this paragraph:

"The individual action of any one club may exert tremendous pressures upon the whole structure of professional baseball, and could conceivably result in lessening the value of several major league franchises."

Baseball law, originally conceived and written by Abraham Mills in 1883, had never contained a line that would bar a black man from playing on white professional teams. And while discrimination did exist, it was based solely on an unwritten understanding among white club owners, players and—to some degree—the public.

Early in 1947, however, the Major League club owners voted 15 to 1 to accept the sense of the report issued by the committee and bar Jackie Robinson from the Dodgers.

The lone vote to accept Robinson, of course, was cast by Branch Rickey.

Luckily for Robinson, the Dodgers and baseball, Albert "Happy" Chandler had succeeded Ken Landis as Baseball Commissioner. Chandler, who was a former Kentucky Senator and Governor, said Rickey came to see him soon after the vote to learn whether he would agree to the transfer of Robinson's contract from Montreal to Brooklyn.

Rickey knew, as did Chandler, that without the Commissioner's support, Robinson would remain in Montreal if he was to continue playing in Organized Baseball.

Chandler knew he would face opposition from the owners and others, but gave his approval without hesitation, paving the way for Robinson to join the Dodgers in the spring of 1947.

Robinson's first year in the Majors, as the first black since Fleet

Dodger shortstop Pee Wee Reese.   **Eddie Stanky.**

Walker, proved to be as trying as Branch Rickey had warned. The whole gamut of racial insults were hurled at him from opposing dugouts and, occasionally, from the stands.

Robinson began his career with the Dodgers playing a new position, first base. In the infield with him were second baseman Eddie Stanky, shortstop Pee Wee Reese, third baseman Spider Jorgensen and catcher Bruce Edwards.

The regular outfield included Dixie Walker, Pete Reiser and Carl Furillo, while the mainstays of the pitching staff were Ralph Branca and Joe Hatten.

As the season got underway, there was considerable tension in the Dodger clubhouse.

At one point, for example, Walker, identified in Brooklynese as "the Peepul's Cherce," asked to be traded rather than continue playing with Robinson. But, after talking with Rickey, Walker changed his mind. (He was traded at the end of the season.)

Others signed a petition opposing the new first baseman. Rickey again intervened, and the petition was dropped.

Among Robinson's supporters were two of the most respected men on the team: Reese and Stanky, both of Southern origin.

On their first visit to Ebbets Field, the Brooklyn home of the Dodgers, the St. Louis Cardinals threatened to strike if Robinson appeared on the diamond to oppose them. But the President of the National League, Ford Frick, squashed the threat by telling the dissident Cards that they would either play or be suspended indefinitely.

A conspicuous face can be seen among the 1947 Brooklyn Dodgers.

Off the field, Robinson continued to face many of the conditions he had faced in Florida.

Though he seethed within at such treatment, Robinson never let up on the diamond. As the leadoff hitter, he pounded the ball for a sparkling .297 average, hit 12 homers, led the League in stolen bases with 29 and was second in runs scored with 129.

And though Robinson was in a new position at first base, his fielding average was, at .989, the best on the club. His remarkable accomplishments that year earned him the "Rookie of the Year" award.

Robinson's play, which excited not only the fans but his teammates, was a major factor in the Dodgers' drive to the pennant, which they won by finishing five games in front of their bitter rival, St. Louis.

In the World Series, won by the New York Yankees in seven games, Robinson played steady but unspectacular ball, collecting seven hits for an average of .237.

Still, when the season was over, one thing was clear: The racial barrier in baseball had been broken.

59 The Black Knight

U NDERSTANDABLY, JACKIE ROBINSON was very much in demand at baseball functions during the months that followed his freshman year in the Majors.

There was, however, an unfortunate side effect: His weight ballooned to 230 pounds. And when the Dodgers finished third in 1948, Branch

Rickey pointed his finger at Jackie and said his slow start was one of the main reasons why Brooklyn failed to retain the Championship.

Actually, once Jackie got his weight down, his performance quickly improved and, overall, turned out to be better than the year before.

Moved to second base after Eddie Stanky was traded to Boston, his hitting was only one percentage point below that of 1947. He also drove in more runs, was among the League leaders in stolen bases and had the best fielding average in the League at his position.

The Dodgers, of course, had other problems that season, the main one being that Manager Leo Durocher left the team in midseason to manage Brooklyn's hated rival, the New York Giants.

To replace Durocher, Rickey called on Burt Shotton, an old friend and a sound baseball man who had managed Brooklyn in 1947, a year in which Durocher was under suspension for conduct detrimental to baseball.

When spring training rolled around in 1949, Robinson took Rickey's criticism to heart and reported in good condition. The effort paid off, for that year Robinson won the League's Most Valuable Player award by compiling the following League-leading statistics:

Batting average	.342
Fielding average	.995
Stolen bases	37

He also drove in 124 runs to place him second behind Ralph Kiner, the leader, with 127.

With a balanced pitching staff that included Don Newcombe, Preacher Roe, Joe Hatten and Ralph Branca, the Dodgers captured the flag, beating out a strong St. Louis club by one game.

In the World Series, they again met the New York Yankees—now managed by Casey Stengel—and again they lost, this time in five games.

While 1949 was statistically Robinson's best year, he was always a vitally important member of the 10 Dodgers teams he played with; teams that were never out of the first division, and that won six pennants and a World Championship.

One of the reasons for the team's success, of course, was Robinson's flaming, competitive spirit and extraordinary physical ability. While he was not a slugger like Ted Williams or Mickey Mantle, he was a steady line-drive hitter, especially dangerous with men on base. He was also a superb bunter, some say as good as Ty Cobb. And, like Cobb, he was daring on the basepaths, constantly challenging the pitchers and threatening to take the extra base on the outfielders. In the eighth inning of the first game of the 1955 World Series, he electrified the crowd by stealing home against the Yankees' Whitey Ford.

In the field, Robinson's biggest asset was his instinct, quick reflexes, sure hands and accurate, though not powerful, throwing arm.

Above and beyond that, Robinson was a team player. Remarkably versatile, he would play anywhere his manager wanted him to play. In 1953, for example, he moved to third base to give another black player and first-year man Junior Gilliam a shot at second. That year he played nine games at second, 44 at third, six at first and 76 in the outfield.

Starting at third the following year, he switched to the outfield to make room for Don Hoak. But, he also played three other positions during the course of the season, excluding pitching and catching.

Robinson's greatest game, by his own account, occurred in 1951 when the Dodgers had to beat the Phillies in the last game of the regular season to maintain a tie with the Giants and force a playoff.

In the top of the twelfth inning, the bases were loaded and the score was tied at 8 to 8. With daylight disappearing rapidly, Philly first baseman Eddie Waitkus drove what appeared to be a sure hit up the middle.

Robinson, playing second, dove for the barely visible ball and caught it as it skimmed above the ground for the third out.

Having saved the game, he won it in the bottom of the fourteenth with a homer off Robin Roberts.

By 1956, Rickey had left the Dodgers and moved on to Pittsburgh. That year, Robinson was traded to the Giants. Instead of moving across the river, however, he retired. He said his legs were gone and it wouldn't be fair to take the money offered by the Giants.

During his playing career, Robinson kept his word to Branch Rickey; he wore an "armor of humility" and turned the other cheek for three years.

After that, he behaved as any other ballplayer. Still, it was his remarkable ability and spirit that made most fans and others forget he was black.

In the years following retirement, Robinson became more and more militant about civil rights. He was particularly vocal about the failure of baseball to increase the hiring and promotion of black managers and front office executives. In fact, because of what he perceived to be unfair treatment of blacks beyond the playing field, Robinson boycotted virtually all official baseball functions.

In 1972, however, Baseball Commissioner Bowie Kuhn, who favored the appointment of black managers, persuaded Robinson to attend the World Series to mark the 25th anniversary of Jack's first year with the Dodgers and to honor him for being the first black player to enter the Hall of Fame (1962).

Robinson's spectacular fielding and his homer off the Phillies' Robin Roberts in the bottom of the 14th inning of the final game won the pennant for the Dodgers in 1951.

As might be expected, Robinson, who was now partly blind and whose hair had turned white as a consequence of diabetes, again made a plea for the appointment of more black managers during a pre-game ceremony.

Nine days later, he died. He was 53.

Baseball records show that Robinson played 1,382 games and batted .311. These statistics hardly describe his worth to the Dodgers and the countless thrills he gave fans as a player. And they fail to tell the story of the unprecedented changes his courage and tenacity imposed on baseball.

For almost immediately after Robinson's first year in the Majors, black athletes began to follow him in rapidly growing numbers — not only into baseball, but into other professional sports, notably basketball and football.

And while baseball had only a few managers representing minorities up until the time of this writing, many would agree with the eulogy given Robinson after his death by the Reverend Jesse Jackson, "The phrase for Jackie Robinson went form black bastard to black knight. And we are all better because a man with a mission passed our way."

60 Last of the Pioneers

BY THE 1950s, Branch Rickey had been in baseball for almost half a century and had twice radically changed the course of the game.

Still, the bushy-browed, cigar-chomping teetotaler would shift the fortunes of baseball one more time, although in a completely different fashion than before.

As the record shows, Rickey was not a man to live in the past. With supreme self-confidence, he always looked beyond today and toward tomorrow. His objective, it seems, was to turn a profit for himself and for those who employed him. His method was simple: Improve the product—baseball.

When Sam Breadon fired Rickey as field manager of the Cardinals in 1925 in favor of Rogers Hornsby, Rickey sold the stock he had gradually accumulated to Breadon for $2-million, and without rancor or bitterness set about building a dynasty that endured for years.

In 1951, following the same pattern, Rickey sold his stock in the Dodgers to Walter O'Malley for $1-million and went to Pittsburgh and signed a five-year contract to become Vice President and General Manager of the Pirates at $100,000 a year.

By then, it was evident that the lifestyle of Americans was changing rapidly and baseball, because it refused to adjust to this change, was beginning to suffer.

Automobile travel was increasing as never before. Boating, golf, camping, bowling—all of these activities were keeping people away from the ballparks.

And then there was television, a new technology that was proving to be both good and bad for baseball. It was particularly hard on Minor League teams operating in the shadow of a big league city, and it was devastating to the weaker Major League teams that shared a market with another club.

In Boston, for example, fans would rather stay home and see the exciting Red Sox than pay admission to witness the second division Braves.

And while there were three teams in New York and two each in Boston, Philadelphia, Chicago and St. Louis, there were none south of Washington, D.C. or west of St. Louis.

The Boston Braves were the first to recognize the problem and have the courage to do something about it: They moved to Milwaukee in 1953. The next year, the St. Louis Browns went to Baltimore to become the Orioles and in 1955, the Philadelphia Athletics transferred to Kansas City. Finally, on the same day in 1958, the Dodgers and Giants announced

Branch Rickey launched the Continental League when the Majors dragged their feet about expansion.

they were abandoning New York—the Dodgers for Los Angeles and the Giants for San Francisco.

These moves were highly successful. But to Branch Rickey and a few others, relocation was only the first step that had to be taken to restore and improve baseball's health. Baseball, it was argued, had to expand and grow if it was to not only survive, but strengthen and widen its grip on sports-minded America.

For a brief period, that argument persuaded the 16 owners to consider establishing 10 clubs in each League, then 12, or even three leagues of eight teams. By the end of 1958, however, it became clear that most club owners were not going to make so drastic a move.

At this point, it was announced that Branch Rickey would soon become President of a third Major League, the Continental.

Initially, the Continental planned to field teams only in New York, Houston, Toronto, Minneapolis-St. Paul and Denver. (Later, it would expand to eight by adding Atlanta, Buffalo and Dallas-Ft. Worth.)

"Another baseball war!" was the first thought that flashed through many minds.

Baseball Commissioner Ford Frick, however, took steps immediately to accommodate the newcomers, saying, "We have a responsibility to clear the atmosphere by laying down requisites for Major League status and for furnishing eligible cities with a reasonable program in an orderly and practical manner without destroying our present structure and without the bitterness and disruption of a baseball war."

In an appearance before a Congressional committee, Rickey said the

Continental would be strong enough in three years to compete on even terms with the American and National leagues in World Series play.

While Rickey was completing plans to launch the new circuit, the American and National League club owners had a sudden change of heart and again began to discuss expansion. Then, "like a bolt out of the blue," as *The Sporting News Baseball Guide* put it, the American League voted to consider establishing a club in the Minneapolis-St. Paul area.

From then on, sentiment for expansion snowballed and by the opening of the 1961 season each of the Majors had expanded to 10 teams and also introduced a 162-game schedule.

When it became obvious that the existing clubs had made a firm decision to expand, plans for the Continental League were dropped.

Even though Rickey lost the battle to launch a third Major League, he had clearly won the war. For not until he forced the issue of expansion in 1959 did baseball begin to live up to its full potential and promise.

Branch Rickey remained in baseball despite his advanced age. After his contract expired with Pittsburgh, he went back to St. Louis and, in 1963, became a special advisor to Cardinal President, August "Gussie" Busch.

In November of 1965, Rickey was inducted into the Missouri Sports Hall of Fame. While making his acceptance speech, he suffered a heart attack. Three weeks later, he was dead at the age of 84.

Branch Rickey, who devoted all of his adult life to baseball, was the last of the 12 extraordinary men who gave us today's Major Leagues.

They Gave Us Today's Major Leagues

The answers to the questions raised at the beginning of the book are:

- Who established the professional player and team?
  Harry Wright.
- Who established the National League?
  William Hulbert.
- Who established Organized Baseball and the law that governs it?
  Abraham G. Mills.
- Who established the principle of players' rights and the first players' union?
  John Montgomery Ward
- Who established team defense and team offense?
  John McGraw.
- Who established the American League?
  Ban Johnson.
- Who was the game's greatest player?
  Ty Cobb.
- Who established the home run?
  Babe Ruth
- Who established the balance of power among Major League teams?
  Branch Rickey.
- Who rid the game of corruption?
  In his time, William Hulbert, Ban Johnson and Kenesaw Mountain Landis.
- Who broke baseball's "color line"?
  Branch Rickey and Jackie Robinson.
- Who forced baseball to expand?
  Branch Rickey.
- Who contributed most to baseball?
  In his time, Al Spalding and Branch Rickey.

And there you have it: The 12 men who gave us today's Major Leagues.

Index

A. G. Spalding and Brothers, 23, 73
Aaron, Henry, 91
American Association, 27
American League, 68–71
Anson, Adrian "Cap," 16–17, 51, 59–60,
    64, 156
Attel, Abe, 113

Baseball "wars," 30–35, 46–54, 68–71,
    81–83, 101–3
Brush, John T., 45, 71–72, 74, 82
Bulkeley, Morgan, 18, 20, 30, 89
Burns, Sleepy Bill, 113

Cartwright, Alexander Joy, 1, 89
Chadwick, Henry, 13, 20, 50, 78, 87,
    89
Champion, Aaron B., 1, 3, 7–8
Cincinnati Red Stockings
    defeat of, 7–8
    dissolution of, 8
    origin of, 2–3
    original lineup of, 4
    tours of, 5–8
    uniforms of, 2
Cobb, Ty
    becomes a professional, 90
    family, 90, 96
    fights, 99–100
    final days, 137–38
    first hit in Majors, 96
    and the gambling scandal, 128–31
    Hall of Fame votes, 90
    quits Detroit Tigers, 128
    records, 91–92
    rookie year, 91
    signed by Athletics, 136
    signed by Detroit Tigers, 90
    spiking opponents, 96–98
    suspensions, 100, 137
    in World Series, 94–99
Cobb, W. H., 90, 96
Comiskey, Charles, 51, 65–67, 104,
    110–11

Dauvray, Helen, 41
Dauvray Cup, 62
Day, John B., 32, 49, 51

Devlin, Jim, 21–22
Dolan, Cozy, 132
Doubleday, Abner, 88
Dreyfuss, Barney, 74, 84–85, 103–4

Ebbets, Charlie, 74

Federal League, 101–3
Freedman, Andrew, 71–75, 79–81
Frisch, Frankie, 132, 146

Gehrig, Lou, 139–40, 142

Hall of Fame, 88–89
Hanlon, Ned, 43, 51, 60–61, 63, 73
Hart, Jim, 74, 77, 82
Herrmann, August "Garry," 77, 83,
    106
Heydler, John, 105–6, 110, 132
Hornsby, Rogers, 92, 127, 143
Huggins, Miller, 123–24, 151
Hulbert, William, 15–16
    begins baseball reforms, 20–21, 26
    death of, 28
    Hall of Fame candidate, 30
    and the National League
        organization, 17–20
        president, 20
    record of, 29
    sentiments about, 28–29, 78
    signs Spalding, 16
Huston, Tillinghast, 106

Jackson, Jesse, 167
Jackson, Joe, 92, 109, 111
Jackson, Reggie, 143
Jennings, Hugh, 61, 99
Johnson, Ban, 65
    contributions of, 135
    death of, 135
    elected to Hall of Fame, 89
    establishes New York Highlanders
        (Yankees), 81
    faces first challenge, 103–4
    investigations
        Cobb-Speaker, 129
        White Sox, 110–14
    organizes American League, 67–71

Johnson, Ban *(continued)*
  power of, 78, 83
  protests 1924 Series, 133
  re-election as President of American
    League, 99
  relationship with Judge Landis, 131-34
  resignation as President of American
    League, 134
  splits with Comiskey, 104-5
  suspends Cobb, 100, 137
  Western League President, 66
Johnson, Walter, 89, 109, 133

Keeler, Willie, 61, 81, 83
Kelly, Mike, 42, 47, 51-52

Lajoie, Larry, 70, 89
Landis, Kenesaw Mountain, 116-17
  attacks Johnson, 134
  attacks *The Sporting News*, 151
  bars eight White Sox players, 116
  baseball views, 102
  controls World Series, 120
  early rulings of, 119, 132-33
  elected Commissioner, 117-18
  Feller ruling, 150
  feuds with Rickey, 148-49
  fines Ruth, 121
  fines Standard Oil, 117
  Henrich ruling, 149-50
  investigates Cobb-Speaker, 129-31
  powers of, 117-19
Leonard, Dutch, 129-30
Louisville Grays, 21-22
Lucas, Henry, 33-34, 36
Lueker, Claude, 100

McCarthy, Joe, 143, 154
McGraw, Ellen, 58
McGraw, John, 58-60
  death of, 147
  elected to Hall of Fame, 89
  fights Johnson, 79
  joins American League, 68
  manager of Baltimore club, 63
  manager of New York Giants, 79-81
  managerial records, 86, 145-47
  managers developed by, 147-48
  pitching career, 58
  playing tactics, 61
  relationship with players, 146-47

McGraw, John *(continued)*
  released by Baltimore, 79
  signed by Baltimore, 60
  signed by St. Louis, 64-65
  spurns Federals, 101
  suspends and fines Pulliam, 85
  tactics as a manager, 86
  turns professional, 58
  wins first National League flag, 84
  wins first World Series, 85-86
McGraw, John, Sr., 58
Mack, Connie, 51, 66, 68, 85, 89, 94, 105
Maharg, Billy, 111, 113
Maris, Roger, 141
Mathewson, Christy, 81-83, 85, 89, 93, 147
Mays, Carl, 106, 109, 120
Mills, Abraham G., 31, 37-38
  author of League Alliance, 31
  author of new National Agreement, 53
  battles Union Association, 34-35
  chairs special baseball commission, 87
  contributions to Organized Baseball,
    37-38
  founder of Organized Baseball, 32-33
  ignored by Hall of Fame, 38
  National League President, 30
  quits National League, 36-37
Mills Commission, 87-89

National Agreement, 39
  differing views about, 33
  proposed by Mills, 32-33
  terms of, 39
National Association of Amateurs, 3
National Association of Professionals, 8-9
National Baseball Hall of Fame, 38
National Brotherhood of Professional
    Base Ball Players, 40
National League
  birth of, 17-19
  expulsions from, 20-21
  founder's philosophy, 25-26
  franchises added, 53
  inaugural season, 20
  problems of, 26
New York Giants, 32, 46, 145
New York Knickerbockers, 1
New York Metropolitans, 32

O'Connell, Jimmy, 131
Organized Baseball, origin of, 32-33

Philadelphia Phillies, origin of, 32
Players, abuse of, 38–40
Players' League, 46–48, 50–53
Pulliam, Harry C., 82–83

Reach, Al, 32, 68, 74
Reese, Pee Wee, 163
Reserve clause, 33–34, 38–39
Rickey, Branch, 125
    with the Cardinals, 126, 170
    Continental League President, 169
    death of, 170
    defies Landis, 148
    with the Dodgers, 154–55, 166
    and George Sisler, 104
    and Jackie Robinson, 158–60
    managing career, 126–27
    originator of the farm system, 124–25
    with Pittsburgh, 166
    playing career, 125
Robinson, Jackie, 157–58
    death of, 167
    first World Series, 164
    first year in Majors, 162–64
    greatest game, 166
    marriage of, 160
    with Montreal, 161–62
    playing ability, 165–66
    retirement of, 166
    Rookie of the Year, 164
    seasonal record of, 165
    signed by Montreal, 160
    steals home in World Series, 166
Robinson, Rachel, 160–61
Robinson, Wilbert, 61, 64
Robison, Frank, 64, 71, 73–74
Rogers, John I., 49, 76
Root, Charley, 143–45
Rose, Pete, 91
Rothstein, Arnold, 113–15
Ruppert, Jake, 106, 124, 134–35
Ruth, Babe, 106–7
    benched, 123–24
    with the Boston Braves, 154
    death of, 154
    defies Landis, 121
    final game, 154
    lifestyle, 122–23
    in Minors, 107
    records, 138–43
        compared, 92

Ruth, Babe *(continued)*
    home runs, 106–7
    salary, 152
    walks, 143
    Red Sox career, 107–9
    rookie season in Majors, 107
    sale to Yankees, 109
    seeks manager's job, 152–54
    signs first contract, 107
    World Series, 139, 142–44
        his first, 108–9
        his first with the Yankees, 120
        in 1926, 127

Salaries, classification of, 45
Sisler, George, 103–4
Soden, Arthur, 39, 71–72, 74, 82
Spalding, Albert G., 10, 12–13
    and A.G. Spalding and Brothers, 23–24
    and Abraham Mills, 37
    and Andrew Freedman, 75
    arranges tour of England, 14
    becomes professional, 11
    and the Brotherhood, 51
    Chicago record, 23
    contributions of, 77–78
    death of, 78
    "elected" National League President, 77
    enters Hall of Fame, 89
    joins Boston Red Stockings, 12
    joins first team, 10–11
    and King Kelly, 52
    manages Chicago, 16
    motto, 24
    organizes world tour, 44–45
    pitching record, 12
    rescues Giants, 51
    and the syndicate, 73–78
    and the "war committee," 52–53
Spalding, Harriet, 23, 44
Spalding, J. Walter, 23, 72
Spalding, Mary, 23
Speaker, Tris, 36, 89, 128
Spink, Alfred H., 27
Stanky, Eddie, 163
Stengel, Casey, 146, 148
Stovey, George, 156
Sweeney, Charles, 34

Temple Cup, 64
Tener, John, 105

Terry, Bill, 146–47
Ty Cobb Day, 137

Wagner, Honus, 80, 84, 89, 92, 95
Walker, Dixie, 163
Walker, Fleet, 155–56
Walker, Weldy, 155–56
Ward, John Montgomery
  activities and views of, 40–43
  background of, 40–41
  buys Boston Braves, 54
  death of, 54
  degrees earned, 41
  delivers manifesto, 48–49
  and players' revolt, 46–49
  as playing manager, 44, 46
  record of, 40–41
  refuses to be traded, 46
Wood, Joe, 129
World Series, 84–85, 94–95, 110, 127, 133,
  143–45, 155, 165

Wright, George, 1, 4, 8–9, 44, 89
Wright, Harry, 11
  becomes a hero, 6
  in Boston, 8
  championships, 22
  and convictions about baseball, 4–5
  death of, 55–56
  and the first baseball team, 1
  and first pro league, 9
  managing style of, 13
  with the Phillies, 55
  signs professionals, 3
  signs Spalding, 11
  spurns Brotherhood, 51
  tactics, 13
  tributes to, 56–57
  and William Hulbert, 17, 18
Wright, Sam, 1

Young, Nicholas, 20, 42–43, 76

About the Author

JOHN M. ROSENBURG has been a baseball buff as long as he can remember. When he was a newspaperman in New York, he wrote a column called "Great Moments in Sports," most of which involved baseball. In those days, he also wrote many stories about Broadway and TV personalities. Of Rosenburg's four previous sport books, the one most widely known is his award-winning and best-selling THE STORY OF BASEBALL, published by Random House. Theoretically retired, Rosenburg and his wife live near Philadelphia.